CREATE CRUCIAL INSIGHT

USE DIRECT OUTCOMES CHECKLISTS.
THINK WELL. DO GREAT.

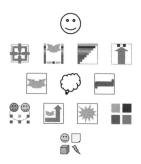

THOMAS J. BUCKHOLTZ

T. J. Buckholtz & Associates
Portola Valley, California
USA

Create Crucial Insight
Use Direct Outcomes checklists. Think well. Do great.

Direct Outcomes publication 4.1.001

Copyright © 2011 by Thomas J. Buckholtz

All rights reserved. This book may not be reproduced in whole or in part, in any form, without written permission, except for the purpose of communicating with the author. Permission is granted for limited quotation in news publications or scholarly publications with the customary acknowledgment of the source and copyright. Inquiries should be addressed to the author.

At the time this edition was published,
- The author could be reached via e-mail at Thomas.J.Buckholtz@gmail.com
- The author had a website at http://thomasjbuckholtz.wordpress.com.

Your use of the material (whether in electronic, print, or other form) in this book is limited by copyright and potentially by other restrictions or agreements.
- For example, you may have received this material based on an agreement between the publisher or author and a workshop provider, personal coach, executive coach, or enterprise or other entity for which you work.

Published by
T. J. Buckholtz & Associates
Portola Valley, California USA

Printed by
CreateSpace
Charleston, South Carolina

LCCN: 2011917403

Table of Contents

Preface v
Dedication vii
Acknowledgments vii
Notice viii

Part 1   Get Results 1

    Chapter 1   Meet Insight 3
    Chapter 2   Play 2-Brains 5
    Chapter 3   Augment Luck 9
    Chapter 4   Create Insight 13
    Chapter 5   Track Results 23
    Chapter 6   Track Utilization 25

Part 2   Learn Checklists 27

    Chapter 7   State Synergies 29
    Chapter 8   State Impact 33
    Chapter 9   State Progress 37
    Chapter 10   State Styles 41
    Chapter 11   State Purposes 45
    Chapter 12   State Assumptions 49
    Chapter 13   State Teamwork 53
    Chapter 14   State Tendencies 57
    Chapter 15   State Inventiveness 61
    Chapter 16   State Drive 65
    Chapter 17   State Resources 69

Part 3   Learn More 73

    Chapter 18   Foster Win-Win 75
    Chapter 19   Detail Opportunities 79
    Chapter 20   Describe Capabilities 83
    Chapter 21   Teach Methods 87
    Chapter 22   Create Metrics 89
    Chapter 23   Create Methods 95
    Chapter 24   Meet Author 103
    Chapter 25   Meet Book 105

Preface

To thrive, or not to thrive, insight makes a difference. People use insight to be aware, to plan, to achieve, and to appreciate achievements. Needs for crucial insight range from personal to global.

I have had the good fortune to create useful insight and to help convert insight into practical benefits for many people.

- Sometimes, I provided crucial insight. For example,
    - When people opposed efforts to develop a city's coastline and parkland, I proposed that the people work to create a wildlife preserve. People other than me established the Palos Verdes Estates Shoreline Preserve (in southern California, USA).
- Sometimes, I implemented other people's insight. For example,
    - A company hired me to lead a corporate-wide grassroots innovation program. The program included the company's first use of personal computers. People assumed the company might not have sufficient software budget. The person who hired me provided pivotal insight by suggesting trying to obtain company-wide licenses to use software. I negotiated such agreements with suppliers. I may have pioneered the corporate software license concept for the world software marketplace. Based on the software licenses and an ample hardware budget, the company could afford to acquire much technology. For some time, the company owned about 0.1% of the world's personal computers. More importantly, numerous employees turned their insights into work improvements. People estimated annual cost savings equal to about 1.5% of annual company revenue.

Part of that good fortune includes having the necessity and luxury to do the following.

- Innovate.
- Think about how to innovate better.

Over time, I developed checklists through which people can create crucial insight. In retrospect, I wish I had had and used such checklists earlier.

I offer you the opportunity to use and benefit from Direct Outcomes checklists. Be apt. Improve your thinking skills. Think well. Create crucial insight. Use the insight. Do great.

If you would like, help other people benefit from Direct Outcomes. If you would like, tell me about successes your colleagues and you create via Direct Outcomes.

- Thomas J. Buckholtz

Portola Valley, California USA
August 2011

Dedication

To Helen Buckholtz
And, in memory of Joel and Sylvia J. Buckholtz

Acknowledgments

Many people contributed to my developing Direct Outcomes and previous books. The following people provided crucial insight for this book.
- Tony Abbis
- Martin R. Radley
- A.C. Ross
- Bruce Tow

Notice

> **Notice**
>
> You are responsible for uses you make of this book and of the information in this book.
>
> Entities providing this book shall not be responsible for uses made of the book or of information in the book.
> - Such entities include the author, the publisher, and any other entities offering or promoting use of this work.
> - No such entity shall be responsible for any decisions, actions, errors, omissions, or damages arising out of use of this work.
> - The author does not guarantee the accuracy, completeness, or suitability for any specific application of any information published herein.
> - Such entities provide this book with the understanding that the author is supplying information, but is not attempting to provide professional services.
> - To the extent people desire or require such services, people might consider seeking the assistance of an appropriate professional.

Part 1 Get Results

Too often, efforts fall short. People make statements such as the following.
- "We could have achieved …"
- "We should not have tried …"
- "We did not think adequately well."
- "We did not work together adequately well."
- "We could have communicated better."
- "We did not have adequate capabilities."
- "We lost focus."

This book provides ways to avoid or minimize such negative results. This book provides ways to create or enhance positive results.

This part of the book introduces the following opportunities.
- Use insight. Thrive. Learn that people use Direct Outcomes checklists to create crucial insight.
- Play a game. Develop themes for marketing messages. Learn how Direct Outcomes can help.
- Anticipate augmenting luck and reducing reliance on luck. Learn how Direct Outcomes can help.
- Use the Create Insight technique. Create crucial insight. Use Direct Outcomes checklists.
- Use the Track Results technique. Anticipate and summarize impact of using Direct Outcomes.
- Use the Track Utilization technique. Anticipate and summarize progress at learning and using Direct Outcomes.

Chapter 1   Meet Insight

Use insight. Thrive. Learn that people use Direct Outcomes checklists to create crucial insight.

To thrive, or not to thrive, insight makes a difference. People use insight to be aware, to plan, to achieve, and to appreciate achievements.

To create crucial insight, or not to create crucial insight, thinking makes a difference. People can treat thinking as a skill. People can use Direct Outcomes checklists to do the following.

- Be apt. Improve thinking skills.
- Think well. Create crucial insight.
- Do great. Thrive.

Figure 1 depicts these three Direct Outcomes themes.

Figure 1   Direct Outcomes themes

Examples: Achieve success via Direct Outcomes

The following statements summarize successes achieved via Direct Outcomes. (In some statements, I changed the names of checklists to [current names].)

- I have used [State Progress] in shifting from a paper-based publication to Web publication and knowledge management strategy. [State Progress] has sharpened my perception of organizations and how they operate.
  - Wayne Hanson, Senior Executive Editor, Center for Digital Government, e.Republic, Inc.
- I recommend the [State Progress] technique for any business executive who understands the value of effective communication and decision making. … Having a simple structure to work with has proven invaluable. I recommend taking the time to discover this valuable tool for yourself.
  - Mike Grove, CEO, Open Country
- I was looking for help in how best to develop a business strategy. Tom Buckholtz introduced me to Direct Outcomes; and through working with the [State Styles] and [State Progress] tools I was able to tear down the curtain around my comfort zone and rewire my brain's thinking process to determine solution sets and best outcomes. When recently asked to take on additional responsibilities at my firm, I turned to Direct Outcomes to help me prepare a leadership plan that will build support for the financial advisors and help them optimize their services to clients.
  - Ronald Mullins, Branch Manager, a global financial services company

- As an Executive Coach, I found Tom's [State Progress checklist] to be extremely effective. This deceptively simple model allows complex ideas to hit home. My clients have received greater clarity due to the model. In one case, an executive who struggled with delegating realized where he was wasting time and more importantly, learned where to focus his time. A second client noted that it was more effective than management books he has read. I love this model for moving clients along their path quickly.
    - Sylvia FerroNyalka, PCC, President, Success Resources Inc.
- The [State Progress] concept espoused by Dr. Buckholtz as part of his [Direct Outcomes] techniques has had significant impact on me while designing our standard-setting Maestro Business Model. What makes it compelling is both its conceptual framework and practical-tool powers to solve business issues.
    - Victor Joshi, Managing Partner, Macho 2 Maestro Coaching LLC
- Tom Buckholtz helped us to shape our value proposition by asking the right questions and by making the right comparisons. Our company's executive summary was much improved. Good advice doesn't require much time in the context of powerful tools. And Tom has a large toolbox with methods that he brilliantly applies.
    - Erland Wittkotter, CEO, SlySE Technologies Inc.
- I used the [State Progress] tool to describe how we should structure a technical evaluation of our software by a customer.
    - A student in a leadership and innovation class
- I got the R&D team to understand how working on my project would help its own goals.
    - A student in a leadership and innovation class
- Direct Outcomes tools provide means for analyzing needs for building our coalition and for increasing awareness of possibly hostile coalitions, allowing for contingency planning or outreach efforts. Emphasis in Direct Outcomes on Reuse has made me see this entire endeavor in the context of what will persist once the particular issue of … is resolved.
    - A student in a leadership and innovation class
- A consultant recommended customer- and investor-centric marketing themes and text to a startup, after a one-hour product demonstration and a few hours of work based on one Direct Outcomes checklist. The startup used the themes and text.
    - (I am that consultant.)

Chapter 2   Play 2-Brains

Play a game. Develop themes for marketing messages. Learn how Direct Outcomes can help.

Too often, people miss opportunities to do the following (adequately well or at all).
- Deploy compelling vision statements, messages, value propositions, mission statements, or slogans.
- Convey messages that combine apt practical appeal and great emotional appeal.

Consider using the game *2-Brains: Tell it & Sell it* to help capture such opportunities. Figure 2 provides a guide.

Figure 2   2-Brains: Tell it & Sell it

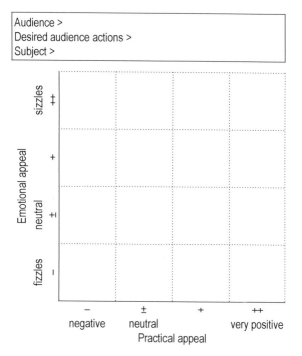

In concept, do the following.
- Use the top area in the figure to do the following.
  - Describe an audience (an individual or group) that a message should motivate.
  - Describe actions people want to encourage audience members to take.
  - Describe a subject (for example, a product, service, societal cause, or business) of the message.
- Use the grid in Figure 2 to record candidate themes.
  - Tell it.
    - Describe aspects of the subject that the audience might interpret as practical.
    - Place those themes. Possibly, use the *emotional neutral* row.
  - Sell it.
    - Develop themes that the audience might interpret emotionally.
    - Place those themes. Possibly, use the *practical neutral* column.
  - Tell it & Sell it.
    - Develop themes that combine practical and emotional themes.
    - Place those themes.

- Rank the candidate themes.
  - Note that people can put themes anywhere in the grid, including at various places within any one of the boxes.
  - Consider moving themes to reflect better themes' relative strengths regarding both practical and emotional. (Generally, a theme is neither purely emotional nor purely practical.) If appropriate, move themes.
- Choose themes. Develop messages.

Example: Learn about Direct Outcomes themes

This example illustrates results people can achieve. Figure 1 depicts three Direct Outcomes themes. Each theme combines *generally practical* and *generally emotional*.
- Do (practical) great (emotional).
- Think (practical) well (emotional).
- Be (practical) apt (emotional).

Example: Develop marketing themes and use Direct Outcomes

Consider using this example to develop marketing themes. Play the game and use Direct Outcomes checklists. Figure 3 provides a guide and a head start.

In concept, do the following.
- Use the first row (*Endeavor >*) of Figure 3 to do the following.
  - Describe a marketing campaign and its purposes.
  - Note an audience, desired audience actions, and a subject.
- Follow the plan associated with Figure 2.
  - In Figure 2, restate the audience, desired audience actions, and subject.
  - Use Figure 3 to help think of themes.
    - Figure 3 contains two groups of columns. Each group has eighteen data rows. The data rows come in trios. Usually, the first row in a trio names a Direct Outcomes checklist; the second row summarizes a category from the checklist; and, the third row is blank. However, the last trio suggests considering methods other than Direct Outcomes checklists.
    - Consider adding methods. If appropriate, add methods.
    - Consider adding categories. For example, learn about a Direct Outcomes checklist and then add categories. (The name of each checklist names a chapter in this book. Consider using that chapter to learn about the checklist.) Add the categories in the blank row in the trio associated with the checklist.
    - For each non-blank Direct Outcomes row, the figure suggests two *emotional appeal* themes.
    - For each non-blank Direct Outcomes row, the figure suggests one *practical appeal* theme.
    - Consider adding themes. Consider adding themes that come to mind spontaneously. Consider adding themes that evoke both emotion and practicality. Considering adding themes based on learning about or using a checklist. If appropriate, add themes. (For the next steps, it should not matter where a theme appears in Figure 3.)
  - Appraise themes.
    - Rate each relevant theme twice. Use the emotional appeal rating scale shown in Figure 2. Use the practical appeal scale shown in Figure 2. Use Figure 3 to record appraisals.
    - Transfer appropriate themes to appropriate places in Figure 2.
  - Choose themes. Develop messages.

Play 2-Brains

Figure 3 Some themes for marketing messages

Endeavor >

Checklists and *Checklist categories*	Themes (generally emotional)	*	Themes (generally practical)	*	Checklists and *Checklist categories*	Themes (generally emotional)	*	Themes (generally practical)	*
State Synergies	Altruistic Power-hungry		Leverage skills		State Teamwork	Spontaneous Forced		Work cooperatively	
Aid peers	Caring Obligating		Build an alliance		*Entities also want …*	Self-aware Aggressive		Be farsighted	
State Impact	Satisfaction Frustration		Know the differences		State Tendencies	Practical Manipulative		Build on proclivities	
Recap essentials	Wisdom Shallowness		Convey the basics		*Useful proficiency*	Beneficial Destructive		Be skilled	
State Progress	Venturing Obsolescing		Follow a roadmap		State Inventiveness	Genius Daydreaming		Catalyze innovation	
Recognize outcomes	Praise Blame		Reward for successes		*Ideate*	Creativity Fantasy		Produce useful concepts	
State Styles	Flair Vanity		Work appropriately		State Drive	Competing Coasting		Align work cultures	
Procedural	Easy Boring		Be efficient		*Striving*	Business-like Panicked		Build new business	
State Purposes	Up-front Devious		Know goals		State Resources	Agile Bureaucratic		Be ready	
Optimize risk-taking	Wise Over-confident		Be prudent		*Reputations*	Halo Pitchfork		Build a brand	
State Assumptions	Wise Guessing		Do fact-checking		[Other method]				
Involve metadata types	Foresighted Technocratic		Enable uses of data		*[…]*				

Remarks

The following statements provide perspective about this example.
- For each Direct Outcomes row in Figure 3, people can think of other themes.
- Each Direct Outcomes checklist has categories not shown in Figure 3.
- People can add and use themes that people do not associate with a checklist.

Perspective

The following statements provide perspective about techniques in this chapter.
- Consider the extent to which people should use systematic methods when brainstorming.
  - *Doing* can produce greater results.
  - *Thinking* can be easier and quicker.
  - *Being* can be more satisfying.
- The game's name comes from the following.
  - People popularly associate human brains' left hemispheres with facts. For the game, *tell it* and *practical appeal* fit with this perception.
  - People popularly associate human brains' right hemispheres with feelings. For the game, *sell it* and *emotional appeal* fit with this perception.
  - *2-Brains* refers to advantages of doing the following.
    - Work with at least two viewpoints.
    - Involve at least two people.
    - Start a name with a number so that the name alphabetizes near the beginnings of lists.
- People can change the grid's axis labels.
  - Figure 4 suggests candidates for axis labels.
  - People can change the candidates. People can add candidates.
  - For an application (*Endeavor* >), people can appraise candidates' suitability based on emotional appeal, practical appeal, and other criteria.

Figure 4 Some candidates for grid axis labels

Endeavor >					
Premises	**++ labels**	**+ labels**	**± labels**	**− labels**	**Appraisals**
excitement	sizzles	crackles	neutral	fizzles	
love/hate	love	like	know	hate	
hot/cold	hot	warm	tepid	cold	
on / off	right on	on	off-and-on	write-off	
positivity	very positive	positive	neutral	negative	
perfect 10	+10	+3	±1	−3	
golf	hole-in-one	birdie	par	bogey	
sporting	win-win	win	draw	lose	
automobile gears	high	low	neutral	reverse	
benefit	very useful	useful	neutral	harmful	
[other]					

Chapter 3   Augment Luck

Anticipate augmenting luck and reducing reliance on luck. Learn how Direct Outcomes can help.

Too often, people miss opportunities to do the following (adequately well or at all).
- Proactively think and thereby do the following.
  - Augment the luck that comes their way.
  - Avoid overly depending on luck.

Consider taking proactive steps to help capture such opportunities. Figure 5 depicts two paths to creating crucial insight. The second path features less work, better results, and happier people. People can traverse the second path more surely, easily, and quickly. The second path also features using Direct Outcomes and relying less on luck.

Figure 5   Luck? Or, Direct Outcomes?

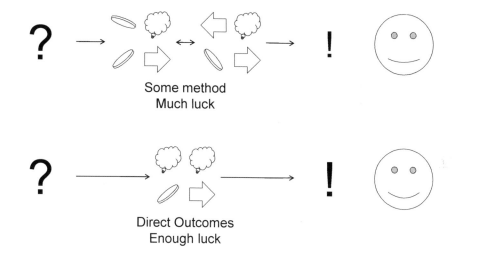

Example: Contrast "with much luck" with "with Direct Outcomes"

This example shows advantages people can gain by proactively thinking and by using Direct Outcomes.

Endeavor

Advise leaders of a political organization. In particular, review operations and suggest improvements.

Situation

Late twentieth century practices of an American political party's National Committee emphasize the following activities.
- Support some office-seeking candidates' campaigns.
- Help build some organizations, such as state parties.

Fundraising supports both types of activities.

During 2000, the organization runs a project to produce a report from the National Committee Chairman to the next cadre of leaders. The Chairman wants to help future leaders sustain and improve the organization. I serve as the main consultant for the project. The project conducts approximately seventy five interviews. Interviewees suggest improvements to existing operations.

Actions

I recommend adding a grassroots line of business. I propose a theme of *winning hearts, minds, and participation of Americans*.

Results

In 2001, the National Committee forms a grassroots program and a grassroots division. One part of the program attracts an online registration of at least 1.4 million *team leaders*.

Remarks

The actual history follows the Figure 5 path that emphasizes luck. Forming the grassroots program depends on much happenstance and my insight. Remove any one of the following actions. The National Committee does not create the program. (Possibly, the Committee creates a similar program later.)

- The project manager learns of me.
- The manager visits me in California.
- The manager and I agree I will work on the project.
- I make an out-of-scope recommendation (regarding *winning hearts, minds, and participation of Americans*).
  - People expect the report to cover traditional operations.
- The manager embraces the recommendation.
- The manager features the recommendation in the report.

The second path symbolizes promise associated with Direct Outcomes. People can produce similar or better results more surely, easily, and quickly.

The left column of Figure 6 shows questions that pertain to endeavors. The figure also lists the eleven Direct Outcomes checklists and provides a symbol for each checklist. People can use each checklist to help answer the corresponding question. (Note: For an endeavor, more questions can pertain. Potentially, people can use each checklist to help answer each question.)

Figure 6 From some questions to some applicable checklists

Endeavor [>]

To What Extent Does the Endeavor Appropriately ...	Examples of Checklists
Coordinate with other endeavors?	State Synergies
Declare the value it creates for constituents?	State Impact
Progress toward creating value?	State Progress
Accomplish work?	State Styles
Declare the endeavor's goals?	State Purposes
Use information?	State Assumptions
Foster teamwork among participants?	State Teamwork
Motivate participants?	State Tendencies
Consider participants' innovation proclivities?	State Inventiveness
Consider participants' drive?	State Drive
Attract participants and other resources?	State Resources

On the second path, people can generate the grassroots program concept - and potentially additional useful insight - without much of the happenstance in the actual history. The following actions can occur.
- People read a list of Direct Outcomes checklists. The first checklist carries the name State Synergies.
- People discover the grassroots program concept. Any one of the following ways suffices. Other similar ways can work. Only one way need occur.
  - People think about implications of the checklist's name, State Synergies.
  - People apply the checklist and derive the concept from the second of the checklist's five categories. That category suggests, "Aid peers." The following activities occur.
    - People consider donors and other activists to be peers.
    - People ask, "How can these peers aid each other?"
    - People think, "A grassroots program can help."
  - People apply the checklist and derive the concept from the third of the checklist's categories. That category suggests, "Help providers." The following activities occur.
    - People consider donors and other activists to be providers to the National Committee.
    - People ask, "How can the National Committee aid these providers?"
    - People think, "A grassroots program can help."
  - People apply Figure 6 and derive the concept. The following activities occur.
    - People define *endeavor* as *the National Committee conducts its business*.
    - People read the figure's first question.
    - People think of endeavors of donors and other activists.
    - People ask, "How can the National Committee aid those endeavors?"
- People add *start a grassroots program* to the list of possible improvements.
- People continue to work with State Synergies and other Direct Outcomes checklists. Possibly,
  - People discover other candidate improvements.

- People hone their concepts for candidate improvements.
- People document, prioritize, and pursue candidate improvements.

Perspective

This section provides perspective about needs for, and advantages of using, Direct Outcomes.

Situation

People want their endeavors to achieve great results. People want to benefit from other people's endeavors. Perhaps people want other individuals to benefit from the people's endeavors. People want to minimize unneeded effort, delay, and use of resources.

- Here, *endeavor* denotes any activity, program, project, or task. Generally, human endeavors have (or formulate) and pursue purposes or goals. Examples of endeavors include the following.
  - People work to eradicate polio worldwide.
  - An organization tries to develop and implement a strategic plan.
  - An enterprise attempts to develop and offer a new product or service.
  - A team tries to complete a project.
  - A company or individual works to improve processes or metrics.
  - A group writes a document.
  - People attempt to frame an issue (or pinpoint a problem or create an opportunity) or act based on direction thus set.

Results

Figure 7 summarizes results people can achieve by using Direct Outcomes.

Figure 7   Results people can achieve by using Direct Outcomes

Generally	Specifically
Society and people's endeavors can thrive because people generate crucial insight by using Direct Outcomes checklists.	Create breakthroughs people need. Use Direct Outcomes. Generate crucial insight. Use the insight. Gain impact. Save time. Thrive.

Consider applying Direct Outcomes to work having goals such as the following.
- Gain impact and save time - in almost any effort.
- Benefit from crucial insight.
- Increase possibilities that people explore diverse useful alternatives.
- Reduce possibilities and risks that people generate insight that is too insufficient or too late.
- Increase confidence that people know the extent to which they have done enough work.

Remarks

The next chapter of this book provides a method for using Direct Outcomes.

Chapter 4   Create Insight

Use the Create Insight technique. Create crucial insight. Use Direct Outcomes checklists.

Too often, people miss opportunities to do the following (adequately well or at all).
- Create useful concepts or options that otherwise might be overlooked.
- Crosscheck plans or metrics for thoroughness or consistency.
- Estimate or articulate the value endeavors generate.
- Help people utilize common bases for communicating and cooperating.
- Organize the content of communications.
- Help perform many other business-like activities.
- Learn, use, and benefit from Direct Outcomes. Specifically,
    - Create crucial insight.
        - Examples might include concepts for practical goals, products, alliances, and activities.
    - Estimate the extent to which people explore a robust set of alternative courses of action.
    - Use insight well.
    - Help people learn and use Direct Outcomes.

Consider using this technique to help capture such opportunities. Figure 8 provides a guide. The following numbered list outlines a method. (This chapter's *Example* section provides an example. This chapter's *Perspective* section provides further information. That information tracks the method. To use the method, people may need at most just some of that information.)

Figure 8   Create Insight

Endeavor >				
Aspects (of the endeavor)	Plans and Actions to Analyze Aspects	Plans and Actions to Perform Aspects	Checklists (that plans specify or actions use)	Insights and Other Results
>	>	>	>	>
>	>	>	>	>
>	>	>	>	>
>	>	>	>	>
>	>	>	>	>

People can do the following.
1. Describe an endeavor of interest to people.
2. Determine, regarding the endeavor, aspects to analyze or perform.
    - Aspects to analyze can include the following.
        - Questions, issues, problems, or opportunities related to the endeavor
        - Activities within the endeavor
    - Aspects to perform can include the following.
        - Activities within the endeavor
3. Take action to create insight about aspects or to perform aspects.
    - Select relevant Direct Outcomes checklists.
    - Use people's repertoires of skills and methods, including Direct Outcomes checklists.
    - Use endeavor-specific judgment.
4. Summarize, announce, and use crucial insights and other results generated.

5. Measure, appreciate, and reuse progress.
    - Estimate the value obtained by using Direct Outcomes checklists.
    - Estimate people's proficiency at using Direct Outcomes checklists.

In concept, do the following.
- Use the top row in the figure to describe the endeavor.
- Use the five columns in the figure to record findings.
    - Use the leftmost column to record aspects related to the endeavor.
    - Use the second column to record plans and actions to analyze aspects.
    - Use the third column to record plans and actions to perform aspects.
    - Use the fourth column to list checklists associated with plans or actions.
    - Use the rightmost column to record insights and other results created via actions.

Example: Brainstorm themes for a mission statement

Figure 9 illustrates one instance of *analyze aspects* and one instance of *perform aspects*. The endeavor includes a step at which people brainstorm to create themes for a mission statement for a business. Text below (not in) the figure describes *Insights and Other Results*.

Figure 9 From some endeavor aspects toward some insights and other results

Endeavor > People develop a mission statement for a business.				
Aspects (of the Endeavor)	**Plans and Actions to Analyze Aspects**	**Plans and Actions to Perform Aspects**	**Checklists (that plans specify or actions use)**	**Insights and Other Results**
The brainstorming step	Anticipate how well people will likely perform the step.	-	State Styles	>
The brainstorming step	-	Develop candidate themes for the mission statement.	State Progress State Styles	>

People do analytic work per the second-to-last row of the figure. People use the State Styles checklist. People develop the following insights.
- If people use traditional behavior only, brainstorming will likely be mostly a *haphazard* activity.
- If people use Direct Outcomes checklists, brainstorming can be more a *procedural* activity.
- In this situation, procedural work is likely to produce better results for less effort and in less time than would haphazard work.

Create Insight   15

People use results from the analytic work to do the work noted in the last row in the figure. People use State Progress and State Styles while performing the brainstorming step. Results include the following.

- Some candidate mission-statement themes emphasize contributions to customers' missions.
  - People discover some of these themes by using State Progress procedurally. In particular, people associate customers' goals with the checklist's *Outcomes / Recognize outcomes* category. Candidate themes feature services addressing customers' needs in relevant State Progress categories. For example,
    - People consider the State Progress category *Actions / Perform actions*. People develop candidate themes that emphasize the ease with which customers achieve their results because customers use the business's products and services.
    - People consider the State Progress category *Scenarios / Build scenarios*. People develop candidate themes that emphasize the ease with which customers decide to engage with the business.
- Some candidate mission-statement themes emphasize contributions to the efficiency of customers' work.
  - People discover some of these themes by using State Styles procedurally. In particular, people analyze how well customers do perform and could perform work. Candidate themes feature services helping customers adjust the styles with which customers to their work.

Perspective

This advice tracks the numbered steps in the method.

1. **The following remarks pertain to endeavors.**
    - People have a wide range of choices regarding scope. For example, the following items represent some endeavors regarding wellness.
      - Improve medical and financial wellness (of people throughout a nation, employees within an enterprise, or an individual).
      - Improve healthcare services (respectively, for people nationally, the enterprise's employees, or the individual).
      - Improve insurance programs related to healthcare services.
      - Write a document describing a specific insurance program.
      - Outline such a document.
    - People can adjust an endeavor's scope or definition. When people do so, they can consider backtracking regarding the method's steps.
    - Figure 10 depicts a model for an endeavor.

Figure 10 Endeavor themes and some endeavor elements

Themes		Typical Activities	Endeavor Elements
Do	😊	Create effects	Effects
Think	💭	Form agendas	Agendas
Be		Shape potential	Potential

Endeavor >

- The following statements characterize the model.
  - The model features three themes - *do*, *think*, and *be*.
  - The following types of activities typify the respective themes.
    - Create effects: Take action to produce results. Measure or appreciate outcomes. Reuse, beyond the endeavor, facets of the endeavor.
    - Form agendas: Use information or make assumptions. Develop alternative scenarios. Choose plans.
    - Shape potential: Gather resources. Motivate participants. Develop teamwork.
- The following statements pertain to endeavor elements.
  - There are four endeavor elements.
    - Figure 10 notes three elements - *effects*, *agendas*, and *potential*.
    - The fourth element is *programs*. Here, *program* denotes a subset of an endeavor. A program includes some of the endeavor's effects, agendas, and potential.
  - Each model theme has a related endeavor element.
  - Potential, aided by agendas, produces effects.
  - Effects can contribute to potential and agendas.
  - Agendas can contribute to potential.
- Figure 11 lists some activities that occur in endeavors.

Figure 11 From endeavor elements to some types of activities

Effects ...	• Work with providers	• Catalyze innovation
• Describe outcomes	• Form coalitions	• Delegate authority
• Measure results	• Structure, merge, or split organizations	• Manage risk
• Achieve results		• Effect financial success
• Other (Specify.):	• Motivate participants	• Create products or services
Agendas ...	• Effect staffing	• Market products or services
• Achieve buy-in	• Effect learning	• Sell products or services
• Communicate intent	• Effect careers	• Negotiate agreements
• Establish direction	• Deploy methods or systems	• Manage projects
• Develop perspective		• Delegate work
• Learn intent	• Free up time	• Accomplish work
• Other (Specify.):	• Other (Specify.):	• Streamline work
Potential ...	Programs ...	• Acquire products or services
• Effect teamwork	• Implement decisions	
• Work with clients	• Make decisions	• Other (Specify.):
	• Effect leadership	

- People can consider any activity to be its own endeavor. For example, a primary endeavor can include projects. People can consider a project to be an endeavor. A project can include tasks. People can consider a task to be an endeavor. People can do the following.
    - Take advantage of this flexibility.
    - Define each endeavor well.
    - Consider the extent to which to analyze separately each endeavor.

2. **The following remarks pertain to aspects.**
    - People can use the questions in Figure 6 to help select aspects or formulate questions.
    - People can select activities that people want to improve, emulate, or eliminate.
        - Figure 11 lists some types of activities.
        - The left column of Figure 12 suggests some types of activities.
        - Endeavors can include other types of activities.
    - People can use the model in Figure 13 to help select aspects.
        - For example, people can consider the *typical activities*.
    - People's aspects may differ from those shown in Figure 6, Figure 11, Figure 12, and Figure 13. For example, some of people's aspects may be more specific.
    - People can list (in Figure 8) aspects in any appropriate - or no particular - order.
        - The order of the questions in Figure 6 arises from Figure 13.
    - People can adjust a list of aspects. When people do so, they can consider backtracking regarding the method's steps.

Figure 12 From some types of activities to some applicable checklists

Endeavor >	
Examples of Types of Activities	**Examples of Applicable Checklists**
Identify entities or efforts that the endeavor affects or that affect the endeavor. Prepare to reuse aspects of the endeavor. Prepare to merge processes.	Use the State Synergies checklist. Spot opportunities for cooperation.
Recognize outcomes and attribute value to them. Compare plans or scenarios. Choose plans to pursue.	Use the State Impact checklist. Evaluate courses of action.
Produce results. Create scenarios. Plan needed activities. Create concepts or value statements for products and services. Market and sell. Understand types of work people do or like to do.	Use the State Progress checklist. Plan and manage services, programs, and projects. Envision new products and services. Develop marketing themes.
Decide the extent to which to change how people do some work. Understand types of work-behavior people use or like to use.	Use the State Styles checklist. Analyze how work is or could be done.
Declare goals. Find and understand factors that motivate people, organizations, and coalitions to participate.	Use the State Purposes checklist. Envision purposes that motivate or can motivate individuals, teams, relationships, and activities.
Identify and hone perceptions. Qualify information. Prepare to gather metadata (data about information collected or used).	Use the State Assumptions checklist. Determine the extent information meets needs. Spot needs for additional information.
Ensure resources work together appropriately. Develop service agreements. Facilitate a joint venture, merger, acquisition, or divestiture.	Use the State Teamwork checklist. Envision and guide relationships between entities.
Identify factors influencing the possibilities for successful teamwork or participation.	Use the State Tendencies checklist. Envision matches and mismatches between needs to do work and behaviors people tend to use when working.
Understand histories and attitudes regarding innovation and innovative work.	Use the State Inventiveness checklist. Envision matches and mismatches between needs for innovation and proclivities of participants.
Understand histories and attitudes regarding competiveness of work.	Use the State Drive checklist. Envision matches and mismatches between endeavor needs or cultures and participants' attitudes.
Involve appropriate resources. Identify inappropriate resources.	Use the State Resources checklist. Determine capabilities needed so that endeavors succeed.

Create Insight

Figure 13 From some endeavor elements to some applicable checklists

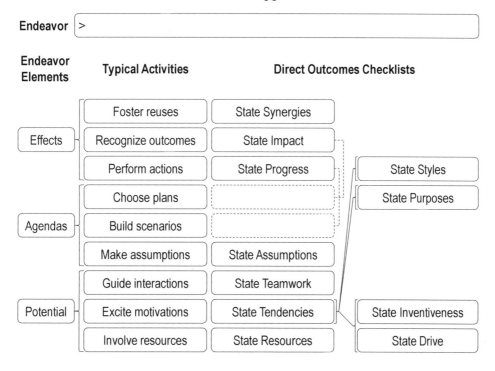

- The following remarks pertain to questions.
  - People can frame questions as "*To what extent ...?*"
    - People may think more usefully and more broadly based on a "To what extent does (or, is) ...?" question than based on the parallel "Does (or, is) ..." question.
  - People can use a word like *appropriately* or *appropriate*.
    - Without such a word, a question can invite people to estimate *what is*.
    - With such a word, a question can invite people to estimate *what should be*.
  - People can combine the above two actions. When people compare or choose among alternatives, the following can occur.
    - People use similarities between the alternatives as context.
    - People use the context to evaluate differences between alternatives.
    - People may decide not to debate further the differences.
    - For such a debate, people may use the context to simplify evaluating the alternatives.

3. **The following remarks pertain to actions and Direct Outcomes.**
   - The following remarks pertain to Direct Outcomes.
     - The Direct Outcomes program embraces principles shown in Figure 14.

Figure 14 Direct Outcomes program principles

- The program applies to almost any business-like endeavor.
- The program includes checklists. A checklist provides categories for which checklist users can state findings or instances.
- Almost anyone capable of business-like work should be able to benefit by using the checklists.
- People can use the checklists to think of possibilities that people might otherwise miss.
- People can obtain useful insight, rather easily and rather quickly.
- One use of one checklist can prove pivotal for an endeavor.
- Each checklist applies to almost any facet of an endeavor.
- The checklists balance usefulness and rigor.
- The checklists do not necessarily cover completely people's needs. People should consider also applying other methods.
- People can use the checklists with - and to add usefulness to - non-Direct Outcomes methods.
- The checklists do not dictate right answers. People should apply situation-specific judgment.

- People can use Direct Outcomes to deploy the endeavor themes positively.
  - People can use *do great* for *do*.
  - People can use *think well* for *think*.
  - People can use *be apt* for *be*.
- Direct Outcomes includes eleven checklists.
- For each checklist, Figure 6 provides a symbol and a name.
- For each checklist, this book has a chapter named for the checklist.
- In some circumstances, people can treat the checklists as being independent of each other.
- People can use combinations of checklists.
- Relationships exist between some checklists. The following note examples.
  - State Assumptions adds detail to State Progress.
  - State Tendencies recommends using four checklists.
- Figure 13 shows some relations between three endeavor elements and the eleven Direct Outcomes checklists.
  - The leftmost column shows those endeavor elements.
  - The second column shows typical activities.
    - For each of the three endeavor elements, the column shows three activities.
    - Such a trio of activities represents a second-tier use of the *effects, agendas, and potential* model.
    - (Note: The nine activities dovetail with the State Progress checklist.)
  - The rightmost two columns name the eleven checklists.
    - The following statements pertain to checklists in the left one of those two columns. Each checklist applies to the activity to its left. Each checklist applies more broadly. State Impact applies well to *agendas - choose plans*. State Progress applies well to *agendas - build scenarios*.
    - The following statements pertain to each of the four checklists in the rightmost one of those two columns. The checklist applies to the activity to its left. The checklist applies to the *excite motivations* activity. The State Tendencies checklist incorporates the checklist. The checklist applies more broadly.
    - The connectors between those two columns group the checklists in the rightmost column according to a third-tier use of the model. This use pertains to *potential - excite motivations*. State Styles corresponds to *effects*. State Purposes corresponds to *agendas*. State Inventiveness and State Drive correspond to *potential*.

- The following remarks pertain to selecting Direct Outcomes checklists.
  - For each aspect people address, the following pertain.
    - Useful applications of each Direct Outcomes checklist likely exist.
    - People likely can generate useful insight by using one well-chosen checklist.
    - People may be able to choose appropriate Direct Outcomes checklists by consulting one of Figure 6, Figure 12, and Figure 13. If not, people may want to use information in chapters in this book's Learn Checklists part.
  - People can gain skill at selecting checklists, by doing the following.
    - Use the checklists.
    - Read this book.
- The following remarks pertain to learning Direct Outcomes checklists.
  - Figure 15 provides a roadmap to this book's chapters.
    - The roadmap applies the model to position chapters.

Figure 15 From Direct Outcomes themes and book parts to chapters and checklists

Endeavor > People benefit from Direct Outcomes.			
Direct Outcomes Themes (Endeavor elements)	**Chapters in Part 1 Get Results**	**Chapters in Part 2 Learn Checklists**	**Chapters in Part 3 Learn More**
Do great (Effects)	Track Results Create Insight		Foster Win-Win
Think well (Agendas)	Meet Insight Play 2-Brains		Detail Opportunities
Be apt (Potential)	Track Utilization Augment Luck	State Synergies State Impact State Progress State Styles State Purposes State Assumptions State Teamwork State Tendencies State Inventiveness State Drive State Resources	Describe Capabilities Teach Methods Create Metrics Create Methods
			Meet Author Meet Book

  - People can learn about a checklist by using the chapter named for the checklist. The chapter appears in this book's Learn Checklists part. The chapter summarizes uses for the checklist, depicts the checklist, notes some opportunities to which the checklist applies, provides a process for using the checklist, and gives examples of using the checklist. The chapter contains the sections that Figure 16 describes.

Figure 16 Structure of a chapter presenting a checklist

- (No section title) - This section does the following.
  - Summarize uses for the checklist.
  - Provide a **Figure** depicting the checklist.
  - List opportunities people often miss.
    - People can use the checklist to help capture such opportunities.
  - Provide a process people can follow to use the checklist.
    - The process description helps define the checklist.
- *Example: Interpret history* - This section provides an example of using the checklist to interpret aspects of an endeavor. The section defines the endeavor. The section discusses a situation, actions, and results. The section provides remarks.
- *Example: Hire salesperson* - This section provides an example of using the checklist.
  - People can consider adding instances to the example.
  - People can consider adding specifics to instances.
- *Example: Foster innovation* - This section provides an example of using the checklist to characterize aspects of a company-wide grassroots innovation program. The program includes use of a new type of information technology.

- The following remarks pertain to using Direct Outcomes.
  - For some applications of some Direct Outcomes checklists, it is important to hold to one definition of endeavor.
    - For example, people can consider making separate uses of State Progress when applying this checklist to a project and to a task within the project.
  - People can use Direct Outcomes checklists to help generate useful endeavor-specific insight.
  - People can use Direct Outcomes to do the following.
    - Analyze what was, is, or would in the future likely be.
    - Envision what could have been or could in the future be.
  - For each use of the checklists, people can do the following.
    - Avoid anticipating that the checklists dictate choices.
    - Use people's overall repertoire of skills and methods.
    - Apply judgment specific to the endeavor.
    - Apply judgment specific to the use of checklists.

4. **The following remarks pertain to summarizing insights and other results.**

   - People can use Figure 8.

5. **The following remarks pertain to measuring progress.**

   - The following remarks pertain to estimating value obtained.
     - People can use the technique provided in this book's Track Results chapter.
       - People can use Figure 17.
   - The following remarks pertain to estimating proficiency at using Direct Outcomes checklists.
     - People can use the technique provided in this book's Track Utilization chapter.
       - People can use Figure 18.

Chapter 5   Track Results

Use the Track Results technique. Anticipate and summarize impact of using Direct Outcomes.

Figure 17 depicts the technique.

Figure 17   Track Results

Endeavor >			
Generic Statements	Baseline Scenario (without using the method)	Differences (impact of using the method)	Significance of the Differences
[This entity] achieves [this result].	>	>	>
[This entity] does [this activity].	>	>	>
[This entity] uses [this insight].	>	>	>
[This entity] creates [this insight] via [this work].	>	>	>
Other (Specify.):	>	>	>

Too often, people miss opportunities to do the following (adequately well or at all).
- Summarize the impact of using methods.
- Help people learn of results people achieve by using methods.
- Inform potential methods users of benefits people can achieve.
- Help methods providers improve or market their services.

Consider using this technique to help capture such opportunities. Figure 17 provides a guide. Consider *Direct Outcomes* to be the *method*. In concept, do the following.
- Use the top row in the figure to describe an endeavor.
- Use the second, third, and fourth columns to record findings. Respectively,
  - Describe aspects, assuming the endeavor does not use Direct Outcomes.
  - Describe differences (from the second column) assuming the endeavor uses Direct Outcomes.
  - Describe significance to various stakeholders of the differences.

Example: Declare impact of using Direct Outcomes to help develop a mission statement

This example illustrates using the technique.
- Endeavor: People develop a mission statement for a business.
- Column 1: People develop candidate themes for the mission statement.
- Column 2: People ideate haphazardly. Themes emphasize products and services.
- Column 3: People apply the State Progress checklist, with customers' goals as *outcomes*. Ideation benefits from structure. Themes emphasize contributions to customers' work and success.
- Column 4: People produce more-compelling results. The endeavor completes sooner. People use less effort. The business improves its marketing. Sales increase.

Perspective

People can use this technique when people use methods other than Direct Outcomes.

The State Impact and State Progress checklists underlie this technique.

Chapter 6 Track Utilization

Use the Track Utilization technique. Anticipate and summarize progress at learning and using Direct Outcomes.

Figure 18 depicts the technique.

Figure 18 Track Utilization

Endeavor >	
Styles	**Methods for which Usage Matches the Style**
Procedural - Follow a process to use the method.	>
Tentative - Experiment with processes for using the method.	>
Haphazard - Meander while using the method.	>
Nil - Defer using the method.	>

Too often, people miss opportunities to do the following (adequately well or at all).
- Summarize work styles characterizing uses of methods.
- Help people appreciate progress at learning and using methods.
- Inform potential methods users about how to measure people's progress.
- Help methods providers improve or market the providers' services.

Consider using this technique to help capture such opportunities. Figure 18 provides a guide. Consider each Direct Outcomes checklist to be a *method*. In concept, do the following.
- Use the top row in the figure to describe an endeavor.
- Use the right column to record findings.
  - For each method, do the following.
    - List the method in any row(s) for which the style matches how people use the method.
  - For each listing, consider describing the circumstances of such use.

Example: Declare people's proficiency at using a Direct Outcomes checklist

This example illustrates using the technique.
- Endeavor: People develop a mission statement for a business.
- Column 2: Procedural:
  - State Progress.
    - People use State Progress to develop themes for the mission statement.

Perspective

People can use this technique when people use methods other than Direct Outcomes checklists.

The State Styles checklist underlies this technique.

Part 2 Learn Checklists

Too often, efforts fall short.
- People lose perspective. Avoidable disasters occur.
- People feel "something needs to be done." No one takes a next step.
- People explore "what needs to be done." No one states a compelling, actionable goal.
- People generally know what needs accomplishing, but not how to proceed.
- People identify worthwhile goals or other good ideas. No corresponding endeavor gels.
- An endeavor pursues worthwhile, well-stated goals. The endeavor fails to achieve the goals.
- An endeavor achieves some goals. Results occur too late. Costs exceed expectations.
- An endeavor achieves all its goals. The goals understate needs.
- An endeavor achieves all its goals. Other endeavors produce similar but redundant results.

This book provides ways to avoid or minimize such negative results. This book provides ways to create or enhance positive results.

This part of the book describes each Direct Outcomes checklist.
- Use the State Synergies checklist. Spot opportunities for cooperation.
- Use the State Impact checklist. Evaluate courses of action.
- Use the State Progress checklist. Plan and manage services, programs, and projects. Envision new products and services. Develop marketing themes.
- Use the State Styles checklist. Analyze how work is or could be done.
- Use the State Purposes checklist. Envision purposes that motivate or can motivate individuals, teams, relationships, and activities.
- Use the State Assumptions checklist. Determine the extent information meets needs. Spot needs for additional information.
- Use the State Teamwork checklist. Envision and guide relationships between entities.
- Use the State Tendencies checklist. Envision matches and mismatches between needs to do work and behaviors people tend to use when working.
- Use the State Inventiveness checklist. Envision matches and mismatches between needs for innovation and proclivities of participants.
- Use the State Drive checklist. Envision matches and mismatches between endeavor needs or cultures and participants' attitudes.
- Use the State Resources checklist. Determine capabilities needed so that endeavors succeed.

Chapter 7   State Synergies

Use the State Synergies checklist. Spot opportunities for cooperation.

Figure 19 depicts the checklist.

Figure 19   State Synergies

	Themes	Typical Activities	Instances
Endeavor			>
	Clients	Serve clients	>
	Peers	Aid peers	>
	Providers	Help providers	>
	Past and Future	Change over time	>
	Other Synergies	Affect other synergies	>

Too often, people miss opportunities to do the following (adequately well or at all).
- Reuse results from endeavors.
- Broaden the scope of endeavors.
- Foster cooperation between endeavors or entities.
- Merge skills.
- Merge methods.

Consider using this checklist to help capture such opportunities. Figure 19 provides a guide. Spot synergies or possibilities for synergies. In concept, do the following.
- Use the top row in the figure to describe an endeavor.
- Use the right column to record findings.
    - Consider that an endeavor might feature the following.
        - People try to achieve goals.
        - People try to do work.
        - People try to use skills or methods.
    - Think of clients the endeavor might serve.
    - Think of peers with which the endeavor might coordinate.
    - Think of providers from which the endeavor might receive support.
    - Think of how the endeavor has changed or might change over time.
    - Think of other synergies the endeavor might influence.
    - Describe activities or other findings.
        - For activities, consider stating metrics, statuses, and results.

Example: Interpret history

Endeavor

People try to improve governmental service to the public.

Situation

Government agencies serve the public. Agencies do not coordinate well with each other.

Actions based on thinking *synergies*

People start a national grassroots movement to try to improve governmental service to the public.

Results

Academics publish research. Organizations sponsor conferences. People participate. Journalists write articles. *Service to the citizen* becomes a topic. Government agencies improve services. Improvements span agency boundaries. Efforts reinforce each other.

Remarks

A service improvement illustrates State Synergies categories (Figure 19).
- Clients receive improved service. Clients provide feedback.
- The service-providing agency learns from other agencies that provide similar services. The agency helps such agencies.
- Service-providing people learn characteristics of good service.
- The service improves over time.
- The public, government, the media, and academia build new teamwork.

Example: Hire salesperson

This example shows insight people can gain by using the checklist. Here, an organization tries to hire a salesperson. People can use the checklist to ideate. Figure 20 shows possible synergies people might spot. People can decide the extent to pursue goals and activities such as those suggested in the right column.

Consider trying to use the checklist to think of other possible synergies. Consider trying to add detail to various instances.

Figure 20 An application of State Synergies to hiring a salesperson

Endeavor >	
Hire a salesperson. • Specifically, meet needs of more than just sales work.	
Typical Activities	**Instances**
Serve clients	Employment candidates receive feedback to help them determine whether they want to take this job. Hiring includes the selected candidate and the enterprise setting expectations for each other. Existing workers prepare to welcome and work with a new employee.

State Synergies

Endeavor > Hire a salesperson. • Specifically, meet needs of more than just sales work.	
Typical Activities	**Instances**
Aid peers	This and other hiring efforts share knowledge about employment candidates. This hiring effort coordinates with corporate-internal programs fostering developmental assignments for employees.
Help providers	Salesperson-hiring decision-makers help human-resources staff and systems announce the job opening and find candidates for employment.
Change over time	Lessons learned from this hiring influence future hiring activities. The enterprise hones its skills at balancing between hiring-for-specific-skills and hiring-for-general-potential.
Affect other synergies	The enterprise encourages salesperson candidates to meet with production and financial staff and to anticipate (if hired) helping various people set prices.

Example: Foster innovation

Situation

This example shows insight people can gain by using the checklist. Here, a corporation has a company-wide grassroots innovation program based in part on a new type of computer technology. Figure 21 lists synergies the staff function catalyzing the program develops.

Figure 21 Interpreting an aspect of a company-wide innovation program

Endeavor > A company improves its operations via a company-wide grassroots innovation program, based in part on a new type of information technology. • Specifically, the program-catalyzing staff function develops synergies with other entities.	
Typical Activities	**Instances**
Serve clients	Company employees receive news of people's success and obtain tips about how to use technology. Champions for specific innovations receive coaching, encouragement to help each other, and information technology. Journalists receive information about the program and about the corporate software license marketplace practice the program pioneers.
Aid peers	The company's project-management office enhances its services, based in part on coordination with innovation-program staff.
Help providers	The company's public relations staff receives (and assists regarding) leads to interested journalists. Corporate legal and purchasing functions receive insight about (and assist regarding) dealing in the information-technology marketplace. Technology vendors receive suggestions for improvements to products and business practices.
Change over time	The innovation program evolves to support growth in the diversity and number of champion-sponsored initiatives, needs for initiatives to acquire special-purpose technology, and diversity of useful technology.

Endeavor >	
\multicolumn{2}{l	}{A company improves its operations via a company-wide grassroots innovation program, based in part on a new type of information technology.}

- Specifically, the program-catalyzing staff function develops synergies with other entities.

Typical Activities	Instances
Affect other synergies	The program leader helps the company develop relations with and learn from the chief executive officer of a semiconductor manufacturing-company customer and a person experienced in the deregulation of a marketplace (other than the one in which the company participates).

Remarks

Without use of the checklist, synergies evolve haphazardly. With use of the checklist, the staff function can systematically plan and pursue such synergies.

Chapter 8   State Impact

Use the State Impact checklist. Evaluate courses of action.

Figure 22 depicts the checklist.

Figure 22 State Impact

Endeavor	>

State Impact

Steps	Typical Activities	Findings
9	Recap essentials	>
8	Make decisions	>
7	Declare significance	>
6	Evaluate differences	>
5	Choose metrics	>
4	Find differences	>
3	Find similarities	>
2	Develop scenarios	>
1	Frame context	>

Too often, people miss opportunities to do the following (adequately well or at all).
- Measure results of endeavors.
- Communicate the value that endeavors can achieve or have achieved.
- Use appropriate processes to select courses of action.
- Avoid selecting a course of action without considering alternatives.

Consider using this checklist to help capture such opportunities. Figure 22 provides a guide. Follow the steps. Feel free, at any step, to backtrack. Determine relative merits of at least two scenarios. In concept, do the following.
- Use the top row in the figure to describe an endeavor.
- Use the right column to record findings.
    1. Discuss the context in which scenarios occur.
    2. Describe the scenarios.
    3. Describe similarities between the scenarios.
    4. Describe differences between scenarios.
    5. Choose metrics for further describing differences.
    6. Apply metrics. Use the results. Discuss further the differences between the scenarios.
    7. Discuss the significance of differences. Consider affected entities and endeavors.
    8. Make decisions regarding the extent to which do the following. Analyze further. Pursue various scenarios. Broadcast findings.
    9. Summarize essentials (from the above steps) for later use.

Shortcutting steps 1, 2, or 3 may lead people to do the following.
- Waste time debating hardly relevant differences (step 4).
- Make poor choices of metrics (step 5) and perform other inappropriately poor work (after step 5).

For steps 5, 6, and 7, people can consider using qualitative metrics and quantitative non-financial metrics before choosing financial metrics.

At step 8, people can consider the extent to which to backtrack. For example, possibly people should not make a decision immediately.

Example: Interpret history

Endeavor

A corporation tries to innovate.

Situation

A staff function starts a company-wide grassroots innovation program based in part on a new type of computer technology. This group leads the program. The group also acquires and provides technology.

Actions based on thinking *impact*

The group requests - from each proposed innovation project - a brief comparison of operations *with technology* and *without technology*, an estimated cost benefit, and the approval of a corporate officer.

Results

Employees market proposed projects to their bosses. Projects gain buy-in. The staff function avoids having to obtain capital-expenditure approvals. The corporation achieves cost savings equivalent to 1.5% of revenue. The savings also represent a 5-times-per-year payback on technology costs.

Reuses

I develop the State Impact checklist.

Remarks

The proposal process illustrates State Impact steps (Figure 22).
- Starting at step 2, the following scenarios pertain.
  - Operate with new technology.
  - Operate without new technology (usually, *business as usual*, but sometimes *best traditional means to do new work*).
- Starting at step 5, the following financial metric pertains.
  - The ratio of annual benefit to equipment cost
- At step 8, the staff function makes the decision based on the following.
  - Principles governing the program
  - Information about the project
- Figure 24 (below) and related discussion provide details.

Example: Hire salesperson

This example shows insight people can gain by using the checklist. Here, an organization tries to hire a salesperson. People can use the checklist to ideate. Figure 23 illustrates preparing to decide whether to hire zero, one, or two people. Over time, people can do the following.
- Work more. For example, identify top-prospect candidates.
- Hone scenarios and metrics.
- Evaluate differences between scenarios.
- Make hiring decisions.

Consider trying to use the checklist to think of other possible findings. Consider trying to add detail to various findings.

Figure 23 An application of State Impact to hiring a salesperson

Endeavor > Hire a salesperson. • Specifically, decide how many and which people to hire.	
Steps / Typical Activities	**Findings**
9. Recap essentials	>
8. Make decisions	>
7. Declare significance	>
6. Evaluate differences	>
5. Choose metrics	Metrics include estimated impacts on … • Revenues • Profits • Market share • Customer satisfaction • Employee satisfaction • Sales-staff retention
4. Find differences	If no person is hired, the organization turns away some prospective customers that approach the organization. If one person is hired, the organization … • In the short term, slows sales activities while extant sales staff members help train the new hire. • In the medium term, engages with all prospective customers that approach the organization. If two people are hired, the organization … • In the short term, risks losing sales while extant sales staff members help train the new hires. • In the medium term, engages with all prospective customers that approach the organization and seeks other prospective customers.
3. Find similarities	The existing sales staff will be fully engaged.
2. Develop scenarios	Hire zero people. Hire one person. Hire two people.
1. Frame context	Planning and budgeting require that new hires be on board by the end of the current fiscal year.

Example: Foster innovation

Situation

This example shows insight people can gain by using the checklist. Here, a corporation has a company-wide grassroots innovation program based in part on a new type of computer technology. Figure 24 indicates information the program-catalyzing staff function requires before the staff function decides whether to supply technology to a project. In the figure,

- C> denotes *information supplied by the project champion.*
- P> denotes *information determined by the program staff.*

Figure 24 Interpreting an aspect of a company-wide innovation program

Endeavor >
A company improves its operations via a company-wide grassroots innovation program, based in part on a new type of information technology.
• Specifically, the program staff decides whether to supply technology to a project.

Steps / Typical Activities	Findings
9. Recap essentials	P> Analysis (if the program staff decides not to supply technology)
8. Make decisions	P> Decision as to whether the program staff supplies the technology
7. Declare significance	
6. Evaluate differences	P> Analysis
5. Choose metrics	P> The ratio of annual financial benefit to purchase price of the technology P> Compatibility with the program's principles
4. Find differences	C> Non-financial differences between scenarios C> Estimated annual financial difference between scenarios (usually the difference in cost to perform the function) C> Quantities of new technologies needed for the scenario *operate with new technology* C> Approval, as evidenced by the signature of a corporate officer
3. Find similarities	
2. Develop scenarios	C> Description of the scenario *operate with new technology* C> Description of the scenario *operate without new technology* (usually, *business as usual*, but sometimes *best traditional means to do new work*)
1. Frame context	C> Description of a function the company needs to accomplish

Remarks

Without use of the checklist, the justification process potentially evolves haphazardly. With use of the checklist, the process can evolve within the framework set by the checklist.

Chapter 9   State Progress

Use the State Progress checklist. Plan and manage services, programs, and projects. Envision new products and services. Develop marketing themes.

Figure 25 depicts the checklist.

Figure 25 State Progress

Endeavor	>

State Progress

	Themes	Typical Activities	Instances
	Reuses	Foster reuses	>
	Outcomes	Recognize outcomes	>
	Actions	Perform actions	>
	Plans	Choose plans	>
	Scenarios	Build scenarios	>
	Assumptions	Make assumptions	>
	Interactions	Guide interactions	>
	Motivations	Excite motivations	>
	Resources	Involve resources	>

Too often, people miss opportunities to do the following (adequately well or at all).
- Develop action plans. Delegate work. Measure progress toward goals.
- Specify services an entity or endeavor needs.
- State the practical value a product or service provides to a client.
- Write a mission statement.
- Think of new products, services, or features.
- Develop storylines or outlines for communications.
- Determine types of work people like - or do not like - to do.

Consider using this checklist to help capture such opportunities. Figure 25 provides a guide. List activities or other findings. In concept, do the following.
- Use the top row in the figure to describe an endeavor.
- Use the right column to record findings.
  - Consider that an endeavor might feature the following nine types of activities.
    - Foster reuses. Extend success by using, in other endeavors, aspects of the endeavor.
    - Recognize outcomes. Realize impact the endeavor has.
    - Perform actions. Work toward results.
    - Choose plans. Set direction for implementations.
    - Build scenarios. Develop candidates for plans.

- Make assumptions. Clarify perceptions, including information, that may affect the endeavor.
- Guide interactions. Ensure teamwork to support all of the above.
- Excite motivations. Identify and provide motivations; thereby, foster participation by resources that think.
- Involve resources. Involve resources such as people, skills, information, systems, and funds.
  - Describe activities or other findings.
    - For activities, consider stating metrics, statuses, and results.

For activities, people can make *plan downward and work upward* use of the checklist. Generally, activities higher on a list depend on results from activities lower on the list.

For communications, people can use the checklist to select themes and vocabulary. Also, people can use the checklist to develop outlines. People can do the following.

- Consider themes inspired by each category.
- Consider wording inspired by each category.
- Try to match themes and wording to audiences.
- Consider outlines that flow from *reuses* or *outcomes* to lower categories.

To plan products, services, or features, people can use the checklist to envision customers' needs. People can do the following.

- Set the endeavor so that customers' outcomes rank above the benefits of traditional products.
- Envision services for each checklist category.

Example: Interpret history

Endeavor

An organization develops a mission statement.

Situation

The organization provides information services. It sells technology-based services. The organization serves as chief information officer for its parent enterprise.

People draft a mission statement. The statement features fostering an *information rich environment* for clients. I, the newly hired leader of the organization, review the draft. I immediately think of *information overload*.

Actions based on thinking *progress*

I try to revise the statement to feature a closer relationship to clients' needs.

Results

I develop a new statement. The statement features the theme *information proficiency - the effective use of information to accomplish people's work and achieve organizations' missions*. Operational statements include the following.

- *Proficiency through information* to communicate and implement decisions
- *Proficiency with information* to make decisions and set plans

The organization adopts the new statement.

State Progress 39

Reuses

I develop the State Progress checklist.

Remarks

Mission-statement themes illustrate State Progress categories (Figure 25).
- Clients' knowing they have completed work fits with *outcomes*.
- *Proficiency through information* fits with *actions*.
- *Proficiency with information* fits with *plans*, *scenarios*, and *assumptions*.
- *Information rich environment* fits with *assumptions* and *resources*.
- *Quality products and services* fits with *resources*.

Example: Hire salesperson

This example shows insight people can gain by using the checklist. Here, an organization tries to hire a salesperson. People can use the checklist to ideate. Figure 26 illustrates thinking of customer activities (and results) the organization might want salespeople to foster. People can use such statements to help find, talk with, and evaluate candidate salespeople.

Consider trying to use the checklist to think of other possible activities (and results). Consider trying to add detail to various instances.

Figure 26 An application of State Progress to hiring a salesperson

Endeavor >
Hire a salesperson.
• Specifically, determine customer activities for which a salesperson could or should provide help, at least indirectly.

Themes	Typical Activities	Instances
Reuses	Foster reuses	Customers and our organization market successes customers achieve via our products. Customers benefit from our future products, in part because we learn about customers' use of current products.
Outcomes	Recognize outcomes	Customers estimate benefits they achieve via our products.
Actions	Perform actions	Customers use our products successfully. Customers acquire our products efficiently.
Plans	Choose plans	Customers make effective acquisition decisions efficiently regarding opportunities involving our products.
Scenarios	Build scenarios	Customers develop useful scenarios for use in evaluating the extent to which to acquire and use our products.
Assumptions	Make assumptions	Customers understand their needs and know of benefits they can derive from our products.
Interactions	Guide interactions	Customers use adequate teamwork - internally and with our organization - to support above-mentioned work.
Motivations	Excite motivations	Customers motivate customers' staffs to perform above-mentioned work.
Resources	Involve resources	Customers deploy people and other resources appropriately to perform above-mentioned activities.

Example: Foster innovation

Situation

This example shows insight people can gain by using the checklist. Here, a corporation has a company-wide grassroots innovation program based in part on a new type of computer technology. Figure 27 indicates possible foci for people's attention and discussion. In the figure,
- 3> denotes the dominant focus (*technology*) that I (the program staff leader) originally observe.
- 1>, 2>, and 3> denote respectively *results*, *human infrastructure*, and *technology* foci I advocate people emphasize - in that order.
- o> denotes other foci that match the checklist's themes.

Figure 27 Interpreting an aspect of a company-wide innovation program

Endeavor >
A company improves its operations via a company-wide grassroots innovation program, based in part on a new type of information technology.
• Specifically, the leader of the program-catalyzing staff function wants to rebalance the attention people's discussions give to various program aspects.

Themes	Typical Activities	Instances	
Reuses	Foster reuses	Market program successes to people beyond the company.	o>
		Market program successes to people within the company.	o>
Outcomes	Recognize outcomes	Note improvements to company operations. Note cost savings. Note other program impact.	1> (Results)
Actions	Perform actions	Improve results of the company and for its customers. Improve the lives of company employees.	1> (Results)
		Implement innovations.	o>
Plans	Choose plans	Develop plans for innovating.	o>
Scenarios	Build scenarios	Describe possible company operations - with or without new technology.	o>
Assumptions	Make assumptions	Determine bases for potential innovations.	o>
Interactions	Guide interactions	Foster teamwork, innovation, and sharing.	2> (Human infrastructure)
Motivations	Excite motivations	Discuss program principles and other topics that foster motivation.	o>
Resources	Involve resources	Develop individuals' skills.	o>
		Evaluate, select, deploy, learn to use, and use information technology.	3> (Technology)

Remarks

Without use of this checklist, the list of such foci evolves haphazardly. With use of the checklist, people can systematically find and articulate foci.

Chapter 10   State Styles

Use the State Styles checklist. Analyze how work is or could be done.

Figure 28 depicts the checklist.

Figure 28 State Styles

	Themes	Typical Behaviors	Instances
	Endeavor	>	
	State Styles		
	Effortless	Transcend needing and doing	>
	Embedded	Blend into other work	>
	Procedural	Follow a process	>
	Tentative	Experiment with processes	>
	Haphazard	Meander while doing	>
	Nil	Defer doing	>

Too often, people miss opportunities to do the following (adequately well or at all).
- Characterize the doing of work. Determine how successful work was, is, or might be.
- Envision alternative ways of doing work.
- Adjust work behavior to improve effectiveness or efficiency.
- Adjust work behavior to ensure appropriate capability or flexibility.
- Anticipate how and how well various change management plans and teams would perform.
- Anticipate the effectiveness - for specific applications - of specific methods or checklists.
- Determine types of work people like - or do not like - to do.

Consider using this checklist to help capture such opportunities. Figure 28 provides a guide. Analyze work styles. In concept, do the following.
- Use the top row in the figure to describe an endeavor.
- Use the right column to record findings.
  - Consider that following pairs - each consisting of an adjective and a sentence - characterize styles that people may use regarding an element of work.
    - Effortless: Transcend needing and doing the work and not lack results.
    - Embedded: Blend the work into other work.
    - Procedural: Follow a process.
    - Tentative: Experiment with processes.
    - Haphazard: Meander while doing the work.
    - Nil: Defer doing the work.
  - For each of various elements of work, list the element with the relevant style(s).
    - If more than one style much applies, consider splitting the element into smaller work units.
  - For each element of work, consider suggesting style(s) the element should match.

Example: Interpret history

Endeavor
A coalition of city residents influences a city's use of its seashore and parklands.

Situation
People submit development proposals to the city government. The coalition works against the proposals.

Actions based on thinking *styles*
A person suggests that there is no end in sight to such development proposals. The person suggests that the coalition develop and advocate a proposal for a wildlife preserve.

Results
The coalition embraces the new goal. The coalition's new approach unifies defensive activities (countering other proposals) and proactive activities (advocating establishing a preserve). The city establishes a shoreline preserve.

Remarks
The coalition's work illustrates State Styles categories (Figure 28).
- Before the suggestion, the coalition's defensive work evolves from taking *haphazard* steps to *following a process*.
- With the suggestion, the coalition *blends* its defensive work into a broader program.
- When the preserve is established, the coalition's work style changes to *effortless*. The coalition takes no further action to conserve the natural resources.

Example: Hire salesperson

This example shows insight people can gain by using the checklist. Here, an organization tries to hire a salesperson. People can use the checklist to ideate. Figure 29 indicates various activities the organization uses to find candidates for employment. The figure indicates that the organization would like to make procedural various methods it uses to find candidates. People can decide the extent to follow plans for changing some ways the organization finds candidates. People can decide the extent to complete analyses.

Consider trying to use the checklist to think of other possible activities. Consider trying to add detail to various instances.

State Styles 43

Figure 29 An application of State Styles to hiring a salesperson

Endeavor >
Hire a salesperson.
• Specifically, find candidates.

Themes	Typical Behaviors	Instances
Effortless	Transcend needing and doing	-
Embedded	Blend into other work	-
Procedural	Follow a process	Find candidates via databases that contain information about previous applicants. • Desired style - Follow • Analysis - No change is needed.
Tentative	Experiment with processes	Find candidates via on-line business and social networks. • Desired style - Follow • Analysis - Changing this work is not a high priority at this time. Find candidates via third-party job fairs. • Desired style - Follow • Analysis - Changing this work is not a high priority at this time.
Haphazard	Meander while doing	Find candidates by asking the organization's employees. • Desired style - Follow • Analysis - Changing this work has high promise and high priority.
Nil	Defer doing	Find candidates by consulting customers. • Desired style - Experiment • Analysis - People need to study implications of such a change before attempting such a change.

Example: Foster innovation

Situation

This example shows insight people can gain by using the checklist. Here, a corporation has a company-wide grassroots innovation program based in part on a new type of computer technology. Figure 30 indicates aspects of work behavior and culture. In the figure,
- P> denotes aspects related to the program and to projects falling within the program.
- T> denotes aspects of practice related to work supported by traditional technology.

Figure 30 Interpreting an aspect of a company-wide innovation program

Endeavor >
A company improves its operations via a company-wide grassroots innovation program, based in part on a new type of information technology.   • Specifically, program participants recognize, respond to, and shape work behavior.

Themes	Typical Behaviors	Instances
Effortless	Transcend needing and doing	P> Work eliminated by program projects
Embedded	Blend into other work	P> Specific elements of work within efforts that require support from multiple information systems
Procedural	Follow a process	P> Some work to be enhanced by program projects T> Much work supported by traditional information systems T> Much work to administer traditional information systems T> Much work within the information-technology department
Tentative	Experiment with processes	P> Some work to be enhanced by program projects P> Some aspects of working with new information technology T> Some work supported by traditional engineering-support information systems T> Some work within the engineering-support unit within the information-technology department
Haphazard	Meander while doing	P> Some work to be enhanced by program projects P> Some aspects of working with new information technology
Nil	Defer doing	P> Some work to be addressed by program projects P> Some aspects of working with new information technology T> Some backlogged work within the information-technology department

Remarks

Without use of this checklist, work culture evolves haphazardly. With use of the checklist, people can systematically identify - and take action based on - traditional and needed work styles and implications of those styles.

Chapter 11   State Purposes

Use the State Purposes checklist. Envision purposes that motivate or can motivate individuals, teams, relationships, and activities.

Figure 31 depicts the checklist.

Figure 31 State Purposes

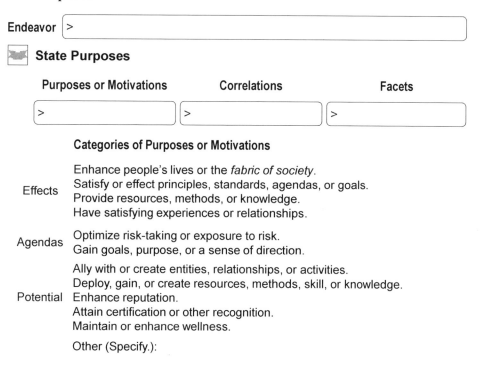

Too often, people miss opportunities to do the following (adequately well or at all).
- Determine or state purposes to pursue.
- Determine facets associated with purposes or motivations.
  - A facet can be an entity, relationship, or activity.
- Determine purposes or motivations associated with facets.
- Correlate - positively or negatively - purposes or motivations with facets.
- Determine facets needed to further - or tending to stifle - purposes of an endeavor.
- Determine purposes on which an endeavor might have impact.
- Measure progress toward achieving purposes.

Consider using this checklist to help capture such opportunities. Figure 31 provides a guide. In concept, do the following.
- Use the top row in the figure to describe an endeavor.
- Use the left area to list purposes or motivations associated with the endeavor or its facets.
- Use the right area to list facets or other bases for purposes or motivations.
- Use the center area to correlate purposes and motivations with facets.
  - For example, consider indicating the extents to which a facet seeks to further or stifle a purpose or motivation.

Example: Interpret history

Endeavor
Understand the purposes of an organization.

Situation
I lead the 2,000-person Information Resources Management Service (IRMS). IRMS is part of the General Services Administration (GSA). IRMS does the following.
- Co-provide the chief information officer (CIO) function for much of the United States federal government's Executive Branch.
  - A unit in the Office of Management and Budget serves as the other co-provider.
- Oversee much Executive Branch procurement of computing and telecommunications.
- Provide information services to the American public.
- Provide telecommunications and professional services to customers within the federal government.
- Perform the CIO function for GSA.

IRMS includes its own multi-purpose staff function.

Actions based on thinking *purposes*
I observe that IRMS serves the following three purposes.
- Provide *service* (and earn money to pay the costs of providing services).
- Provide *regulation* regarding various entities' activities.
- Provide *catalytic leadership* that promotes progress without IRMS's selling services or exercising regulatory functions.

Results
I encourage IRMS regulatory staff to think of regulation as a service that does the following.
- Help clients comply with laws and regulations.
- Help clients take advantage of useful operational practices.

I encourage government employees to find and capture opportunities to provide catalytic leadership.

An IRMS leader proposes that federal CIOs start a nationwide grassroots movement to improve government service to the public. Various people, including me, become early champions for this initiative.

IRMS does the following.
- Reduce the *Federal Information Resources Management Regulation* to approximately one-third its previous word count.
- Increase IRMS's use of advisory bulletins.
- Change IRMS's procurement oversight practices to do the following. Provide more consultation. Focus more on higher risk procurements. Focus less on lower risk procurements.

Remarks
Activities illustrate State Purposes categories (Figure 31).
- The initiative to improve governmental services helps shape the *fabric of society*.
- Emphasizing service aspects of regulation supports *effecting agendas or goals* (government agencies' missions), *satisfying standards* (laws and regulations), and *optimizing risk-taking or exposure to risk*.

State Purposes

- An initiative to train future information resources management leaders helps regarding *gain skill*.

Example: Hire salesperson

This example shows insight people can gain by using the checklist. Here, an organization tries to hire a salesperson. People can use the checklist to ideate. Figure 32 illustrates developing a checklist for people to use when interviewing a candidate. People can decide the extent to use hiring criteria based on activities such as the activities in the right column. In the figure,

- P> denotes a possible positive.
- ?> denotes a possible positive or negative.
- N> denotes a possible negative, to the extent there is a substantial answer.

Consider trying to use the checklist to think of other possible facets. Consider trying to add detail to various facets or correlations.

Figure 32 An application of State Purposes to hiring a salesperson

Endeavor > Hire a salesperson. • Specifically, consider possible goals and activities of a candidate.		
Categories of Purposes or Motivations	**Correlations**	**Facets**
Enhance people's lives or the *fabric of society*.	P>	Enhance society and lives via our organization's products and services.
Satisfy or effect principles, standards, agendas, or goals.	P>	Behave ethically.
	N>	Pursue agendas incompatible with our organization's mission.
Provide resources, methods, or knowledge.	P>	Bring useful perspective.
	P>	Improve our organization's methods.
Have satisfying experiences or relationships.	?>	Travel.
Optimize risk-taking or exposure to risk.		
Gain goals, purpose, or a sense of direction.		
Ally with or create entities, relationships, or activities.	P>	Build appropriate interpersonal relationships with customers, colleagues, and suppliers.
	?>	Participate in a service club.
Deploy, gain, or create resources, methods, skill, or knowledge.	P>	Learn how to thrive in our organization.
	P>	Develop new methods.
Enhance reputation.	P>	Gain credibility with customers and colleagues.
Attain certification or other recognition.		
Maintain or enhance wellness.	P>	Be covered by health insurance.
Other (Specify.):		

Example: Foster innovation

This example shows insight people can gain by using the checklist. Here, a corporation has a company-wide grassroots innovation program based in part on a new type of computer technology. Figure 33

indicates approximate foci for the program's seven principles. The program's staff provides the principles to the company. People use the principles to do the following.
- Determine the extent to get involved in the program.
- Make and explain decisions regarding projects to pursue and technologies to acquire.
- Have a substitute for trying to estimate and discuss goals for the program.

The following statements provide the principles.
1. Meet individual and departmental working needs, both those needs that are common throughout the company and those that are specialized.
2. Deploy easy-to-use systems.
3. Encourage self-sufficiency for organizations and people using technology.
4. Foster integration of processes and technology.
5. Foster flexibility for accomplishing and sharing work and for taking advantage of changing technology.
6. Integrate new-technology-based information into the company's overall information resources.
7. Promote proper sequencing and timing of progress.

In the right column of the figure, a number denotes the correspondingly numbered principle.

Figure 33 Interpreting an aspect of a company-wide innovation program

Endeavor >
A company improves its operations via a company-wide grassroots innovation program, based in part on a new type of information technology.
• Specifically, the program-catalyzing staff propagates principles for the program.

Categories of Purposes or Motivations	Correlations	Facets
Enhance people's lives or the *fabric of society*.		1, 2, 3, 4, 5, 6, 7
Satisfy or effect principles, standards, agendas, or goals.		1, 2, 3, 4, 5, 6, 7
Provide resources, methods, or knowledge.		1, 2, 3, 4, 5, 6, 7
Have satisfying experiences or relationships.		1, 2, 3, 4, 5, 6, 7
Optimize risk-taking or exposure to risk.		2, 3, 4, 5, 6, 7
Gain goals, purpose, or a sense of direction.		
Ally with or create entities, relationships, or activities.		1, 4, 6
Deploy, gain, or create resources, methods, skill, or knowledge.		2, 3, 4, 5, 6, 7
Enhance reputation.		
Attain certification or other recognition.		
Maintain or enhance wellness.		
Other (Specify.):		

Remarks

Without use of this checklist, the development of principles evolves haphazardly. With use of the checklist, people can systematically develop and articulate principles.

Chapter 12   State Assumptions

Use the State Assumptions checklist. Determine the extent information meets needs. Spot needs for additional information.

Figure 34 depicts the checklist.

Figure 34 State Assumptions

Endeavor	>

State Assumptions

Themes	Typical Activities	Instances
Sufficiency	Assume sufficiency	>
Insight	Assume insights	>
Risk Abatement	Evaluate usefulness	>
Knowledge	Evaluate quality	>
Information	Involve data	>
Scope	Involve metadata types	>

Too often, people miss opportunities to do the following (adequately well or at all).
- Guide or document the use of information.
- Help entities do the following.
  - Describe or find needed data.
  - Synthesize information from data.
  - Convert information into useful knowledge.
  - Create or build insight relevant to decisions or action.
  - Estimate benefits and risks of making specific decisions at specific times under specific circumstances.
- Guide the development or evolution of systems that capture, process, or provide data.
- Specify metadata. (Metadata is data about sources, capture, quality, and uses of data and processes.)
- Design information systems so that they record appropriate metadata.

Consider using this checklist to help capture such opportunities. Figure 34 provides a guide. List activities or other findings. In concept, do the following.
- Use the top row in the figure to describe an endeavor.
- Use the right column to record findings.
  - Consider that an endeavor might include the following six types of activities.
    - Sufficiency / Assume sufficiency: Ensure decision makers have estimates of the adequacy of insight for making a decision.
    - Insight / Assume insights: Ensure decision makers (and other people and systems) have key bases - such as principles, knowledge, and assumptions - upon which to make (and implement) a decision.

- Risk Abatement / Evaluate usefulness: Ensure people (and systems) know the extent to which perceived knowledge is likely useful.
- Knowledge / Evaluate quality: Ensure people (and systems) know the extent to which perceived knowledge is likely intrinsically sound.
- Information / Involve data: Amass, synthesize, and offer information (including data and metadata).
- Scope / Involve metadata types: Select types of metadata - topics, words and phrases, authors, date ranges (such as publication dates or recording dates), sources, quality standards, security levels, prior usage, and so forth - that aid in finding or using data.
    - Describe activities or other findings.
        - For activities, consider stating metrics, statuses, and results.

For activities, consider making *plan downward and work upward* use of the checklist. Generally, activities higher on a list depend on results from activities lower on the list.

Example: Interpret history

Endeavor

Improve online information-search services.

Situation

To use an early twenty-first century online search service, a person does the following.
- Input words that might be in documents that might be available online.
- Try to select - from a list of possibly useful sources - sources of data.
- Find - within selected sources - possibly useful information.
- Determine relevance, accuracy, usefulness, and other attributes of such information.

Actions based on thinking *assumptions*

Information-services organizations can try to do the following.
- Accommodate search requests phrased as, "*I want to accomplish [this] in my life*."
- Rank suggested information by usefulness in client-specific contexts.

Results

Over time, the working relationships between clients and information services shift as follows.
- Services shift from dialog based on the services' data to dialog based on the sufficiency - for clients' purposes - of knowledge clients have.
- Services, in effect, evolve from *clerk services* based on characteristics of data to *librarian services* based on needs of a client.

Remarks

Aspects illustrate State Assumptions categories (Figure 34).
- People generally would like to know *sufficiency* - for purposes of making specific decisions - of *insights*.
- People might also like to know the *risk* inherent in using underlying *knowledge*.

State Assumptions 51

- Improvements in early twenty-first century search can feature improvements regarding *metadata* and include an evolution from data-supply-centric metadata (such as words that might be in documents) toward client-demand-centric metadata (such as clients' possible work goals).

Example: Hire salesperson

This example shows insight people can gain by using the checklist. Here, an organization tries to hire a salesperson. People can use the checklist to ideate. Figure 35 indicates possible activities (and results). People can decide the extent to pursue activities (and results) such as those suggested in the right column.

Consider trying to use the checklist to think of other possible activities (and results). Consider trying to add detail to various activities (and results).

Figure 35 An application of State Assumptions to hiring a salesperson

Endeavor > Hire a salesperson. • Specifically, prepare to select a preferred candidate.		
Themes	Typical Activities	Instances
Sufficiency	Assume sufficiency	People estimate how confident they are that supposed insight about relevant factors is appropriate for deciding now whether to fill the job and, if so, for deciding to which candidate to make an offer. • *Relevant factors* include customer needs, enterprise needs, the job, various candidates' qualifications and potential, and possibilities for matches between candidates and the job.
Insight	Assume insights	People explicitly determine or implicitly assume insight about relevant factors.
Risk Abatement	Evaluate usefulness	People estimate the extent to which to trust supposed knowledge about relevant factors.
Knowledge	Evaluate quality	People evaluate the quality (for example, accuracy) of information and of assumptions about relevant factors.
Information	Involve data	People find and develop information about relevant factors. • For example, people find data about candidates - from the candidates, general references, former customers of the candidates, and online sources.
Scope	Involve metadata types	People specify types of metadata that people think are needed to point to - or work with - data about relevant factors.

Example: Foster innovation

Situation

This example shows insight people can gain by using the checklist. Here, a corporation has a company-wide grassroots innovation program based in part on a new type of computer technology. Figure 36 indicates possible foci for people's working with information and tacit assumptions. In the figure,

- P> denotes a focus to which the program-catalyzing staff function encourages company people to pay attention.
- o> denotes other foci that match the checklist's themes.

Figure 36 Interpreting an aspect of a company-wide innovation program

Endeavor >		
A company improves its operations via a company-wide grassroots innovation program, based in part on a new type of information technology. • Specifically, in various circumstances people might like to determine the extent to which to act based on information they have.		
Themes	**Typical Activities**	**Instances**
Sufficiency	Assume sufficiency	o> People estimate how confident they are that supposed insight about relevant factors is appropriate for deciding now whether to take a particular action.
Insight	Assume insights	o> People explicitly determine or implicitly assume insight about relevant factors.
Risk Abatement	Evaluate usefulness	o> People estimate the extent to which to trust supposed knowledge about relevant factors.
Knowledge	Evaluate quality	o> People evaluate the quality (for example, accuracy) of information and of assumptions about relevant factors.
Information	Involve data	P> People try to improve and integrate the company's information resources. o> People find and develop information about relevant factors.
Scope	Involve metadata types	o> People specify types of metadata that people think are needed to point to - or work with - data about relevant factors.

Remarks

Without use of this checklist, abilities to work with information evolve haphazardly. With use of the checklist, people can systematically evolve how they - and the information systems they create - work with information.

Chapter 13   State Teamwork

Use the State Teamwork checklist. Envision and guide relationships between entities.

Figure 37 depicts the checklist.

Figure 37   State Teamwork

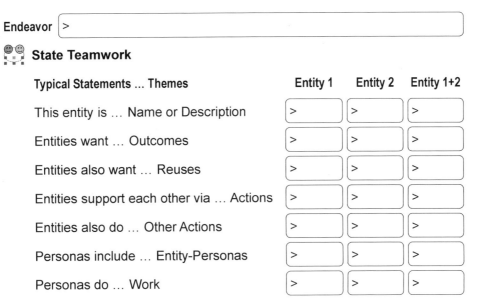

Too often, people miss opportunities to do the following (adequately well or at all).
- Communicate needs or offers.
- Envision or build win-win relationships. Achieve teamwork.
- Help entities support each other. Conduct useful transactions.
- Facilitate joint ventures, mergers, acquisitions, or divestitures.
- Develop or fulfill operational agreements between entities.
- Track progress toward fulfillment of such agreements.

Consider using this checklist to help capture such opportunities. Figure 37 provides a guide. Consider using the column labeled *Entity 1+2* for an endeavor involving a joint venture, merger, acquisition, or divestiture. In concept, do the following.
- Use the top row in the figure to describe an endeavor.
- Use at least two of the rightmost three columns in the figure to record findings.
    - For each entity, do the following.
        - Provide a *name* for or *description* of the entity.
        - Describe *outcomes* the entity wants the endeavor to achieve (for the entity or other entities).
        - Note *reuses* (for various entities) beyond the endeavor that the entity wants to enable.
        - Discuss *support* the entity provides to (or receives from) other entities within the endeavor.
        - Note *other actions* the entity does within the endeavor.
    - For an entity's actions, do the following.
        - Note entity *personas* (and, possibly, their motivations) that take part in actions. (*Persona* refers to, for example, a capability, person, organization, or behavior.)
        - Describe *work* that entity personas do.

Consider - if people are helping an entity 1 and an entity 2 develop a relationship or contract - that, for example, entity 1 may not want entity 2 to know some of the information about entity 1.

For a joint venture, entity 1 and entity 2 form entity 1+2 (the joint venture). For a merger or acquisition, entity 1 and entity 2 become entity 1+2. For a divestiture, entity 1+2 splits into entity 1 and entity 2.

Example: Interpret history

Endeavor

Acquire rights to use software.

Situation

Within an enterprise, the information-technology department acquires personal-computer software for use throughout the enterprise. The department assumes that - in future years - it will not have adequate budget to acquire such software.

Actions based on thinking *teamwork*

Department members work with software suppliers to create a new type of licensee-licensor relationship.

Results

The enterprise and some suppliers negotiate licenses for which the following pertain.
- A supplier provides the enterprise a few copies of the supplier's software and documentation when either of the following occurs.
  - The entities sign the contract.
  - During the next seven years, the supplier releases a new version of the software.
- The supplier has little further obligation to the enterprise.
- The enterprise provides the supplier a single payment for the perpetual right to copy the software and use the software (including upgrades) on any number of computers, but only for the business of the enterprise.

Later, the enterprise estimates it saved - on each of its twelve such contracts - 90% of list price (not including savings on upgrades).

These agreements - and subsequent publicity - pioneer and help establish the *corporate license* (or *enterprise license*) for the world software marketplace.

Remarks

This scenario illustrates State Teamwork categories (Figure 37).
- The enterprise gains productivity through widespread use of otherwise unaffordable software. (*Entities also want ... reuses*)
- A supplier can consider these arrangements as more profit-oriented and less revenue-oriented than traditional deals. (*Entities want ... outcomes*)

Figure 39 (below) and related discussion provide details.

State Teamwork 55

Example: Hire salesperson

This example shows insight people can gain by using the checklist. Here, an organization tries to hire a salesperson. People can use the checklist to ideate. Figure 38 indicates topics that a contract - between an organization and a staffing firm engaged to aid in the search for candidates - might cover. People can decide the extent to pursue plans such as those suggested in the rightmost two columns.

Consider trying to use the checklist to think of other possible topics. Consider trying to add detail to various topics.

Figure 38 An application of State Teamwork to hiring a salesperson

\multicolumn{3}{l}{Endeavor > Hire a salesperson. • Specifically, engage a staff-search firm to help find candidates.}

Typical Statements	Entity 1	Entity 2
This entity is … Name of Description	The provider is … • [name of staff-search firm]	The client is … • [name of organization]
Entities want … Outcomes	The provider wants to … • Earn fees. • Satisfy the client.	The client wants to … • Hire an appropriate salesperson. • Contain costs.
Entities also want … Reuses	The provider wants to gain … • Reputation • Other business with the client	The client wants to gain … • Potential for growth in sales, revenues, and profitability
Entities support each other via … Actions	The provider provides the client with … • Means to hone expectations about the job and qualifications • Access to qualified candidates	The client provides the provider with … • Expectations regarding the job and candidates' qualifications • Funding
Entities also do … Other Actions	The provider … • Engages services of partner staff-search firms.	The client … • Conducts a project to bring on board a successful candidate.
Personas include … Entity-Personas	Relevant provider personas include … • Job and market analysts • Searchers for prospective candidates • Recommenders of candidates	Relevant client personas include … • Experts about work and relationships the job needs to satisfy • Staff who inform the provider regarding acceptances and rejections of candidates
Personas do … Work	Provider personas … • Conduct research. • Screen candidates. • Make recommendations.	Client personas … • Provide data. • Interview and rate candidates. • Negotiate with candidates. • Make hiring decisions. • Keep the provider informed.

Example: Foster innovation

Situation

This example shows insight people can gain by using the checklist. Here, a corporation has a company-wide grassroots innovation program based in part on a new type of computer technology. Figure 39 indicates aspects of the company's relationship with a provider of software. In the figure,
- A> denotes actual aspects of the relationship.
- N> denotes aspects of traditional practice that the provider deemphasizes in this relationship.

Figure 39 Interpreting an aspect of a company-wide innovation program

Endeavor >
A company improves its operations via a company-wide grassroots innovation program, based in part on a new type of information technology.   • Specifically, the company and a software provider administer a corporate software license.

Typical Statements	Entity 1	Entity 2
This entity is … Name of Description	The provider is … A> [name of the licensor]	The client is … A> [name of the licensee]
Entities want … Outcomes	The provider wants to … A> Satisfy the client. A> Earn profits. N> Earn continuing revenues.	The client wants to … A> Acquire the use of useful software. A> Contain costs.
Entities also want … Reuses	The provider wants to gain … A> Reputation A> Other business with the client	The client wants to gain … A> Productivity enhancements, based in part on use of the software
Entities support each other via … Actions	The provider provides the client with … A> A license to copy and use software A> A few copies of the software, at the beginning of the license period and whenever for the next seven years there is an upgrade to the product	The client provides the provider with … A> A payment upon receipt of the first software A> Advice about potential upgrades to the product line
Entities also do … Other Actions	-	The client … A> Gets made copies of the software and manuals.
Personas include … Entity-Personas	Relevant provider personas include … (Personas can be inferred from the next category below.)	Relevant client personas include … (Personas can be inferred from the next category below.)
Personas do … Work	Provider personas … A> Collect one payment. A> Provide a few copies of each version of the software. N> Perform on-going marketing, sales, billing, training, and help-desk work.	Client personas … A> Make one payment. A> Receive software. A> Do internal marketing, distribution, teaching, and help-desk work. A> Provide feedback to the provider.

Remarks

Without use of this checklist, perspective about differences from traditional practices evolves haphazardly. With use of the checklist, people can describe reasons for providers to use the new type of software license.

Chapter 14 State Tendencies

Use the State Tendencies checklist. Envision matches and mismatches between needs to do work and behaviors people tend to use when working.

Figure 40 depicts the checklist.

Figure 40 State Tendencies

Endeavor	>

State Tendencies

Themes	Typical Checklists	Instances
Useful proficiency	State Styles	>
Actionable meaning	State Purposes	>
Innovative mindset	State Inventiveness	>
Competitive mindset	State Drive	>
Other	...	>

Too often, people miss opportunities to do the following (adequately well or at all).
- Build, lead, or participate in effective teams or activities.
- Analyze the extent to which people are likely to form effective teams or initiatives.
- Describe work behaviors people tend to use and determine motivation that may be helpful to encourage people to deploy other behaviors.
- Anticipate, diagnose, or address discord.

Consider using this checklist to help capture such opportunities. Figure 40 provides a guide. The Themes column suggests topics for *to what extent* questions regarding endeavor-participants' activities, attitudes, or mindsets. The Typical Checklists column suggests Direct Outcomes checklists useful for exploring the topics. Consider adding themes or topics. For example, people may know of useful themes not mentioned in the figure. Consider adding or changing items in the Typical Checklists column. For example, people may know of useful methods (Direct Outcomes or otherwise) not mentioned in the figure. In concept, do the following.
- Use the top row in the figure to describe an endeavor.
- Use the right column to record findings.
  - Consider that tendencies might feature the following themes.
    - *Useful proficiency* refers to behavior styles that people may deploy.
    - *Actionable meaning* refers to purposes around which people may rally or to motivations people may have.
    - *Innovative mindset* refers to refers to proclivities or attitudes regarding activities characterizing various stages of innovating.
    - *Competitive mindset* refers to achieved success (measured relative to the achieved success of similar entities or efforts) and to diligence in pursuing activities.
    - *Other*.

- Describe instances.
  - Consider stating pros and cons of the instances.

Example: Interpret history

Endeavor

Bring perspective and encouragement.

Situation

I serve as a Commissioner in the United States General Services Administration (GSA). I serve as a Presidential-administration appointee. I have no previous experience as a federal employee. I believe my opportunities include the following.
- Bring fresh perspective.
- Encourage employees to use my perspective.
- Encourage employees and me to use employee's underutilized concepts.

Actions based on thinking *tendencies*

I act on that opportunity.

Results

Some leaders advise me that there are limits as to how much change people can effect. These leaders note the on-going programs of the 2,000 people in the group. I heed the advice. Employees implement some of my suggestions. I support initiatives proposed by employees. Initiatives produce results.

Remarks

Instances illustrate State Tendencies categories (Figure 40).
- People's on-going and new efforts function best via appropriate styles of work. (*Useful proficiency*, as interpreted via the State Styles checklist)
- Many initiatives fit within traditional purposes of the organization. Some do not. (*Actionable meaning*, as interpreted via the State Purposes checklist)
- Staff members and I contribute via *ideating*. People with significantly *instigating*, *inventing*, or *innovating* innovation mindsets pursue new or underutilized concepts. People with significantly *implementing* innovation mindsets tend to stay with traditional programs and projects. (*Innovative mindset*, as interpreted via the State Inventiveness checklist)
- People with significantly *striving* or *competing* competitive mindsets pursue new or underutilized concepts. People with significantly *coasting* mindsets tend to sustain on-going initiatives. (*Competitive mindset*, as interpreted via the State Drive checklist)

Example: Hire salesperson

This example shows insight people can gain by using the checklist. Here, an organization tries to hire a salesperson. People can use the checklist to ideate. Figure 41 illustrates developing a checklist of topics in anticipation of frank, mutually productive discussion with candidate salespeople. People can decide the extent to discuss such topics.

State Tendencies

Consider trying to use the checklist to think of other possible topics. Consider trying to add detail to various topics.

Figure 41 An application of State Tendencies to hiring a salesperson

Endeavor >		
Hire a salesperson.		
• Specifically, prepare to discuss with salesperson candidates specific conflicts with which salespeople cope.		
Themes	**Typical Checklists**	**Instances**
Useful proficiency	State Styles	The legal department and the sales department tend to differ regarding approaches to developing contracts with customers - *procedural* vs. *tentative*.
Actionable meaning	State Purposes	The financial department and the sales department tend to differ regarding pricing - profitability vs. revenue (and hence commissions).
Innovative mindset	State Inventiveness	The production and customer-service departments and the sales department tend to differ regarding inventing and innovating to meet customer needs - *implement* vs. *innovate* (or *invent*).
Competitive mindset	State Drive	The product development department and the sales department tend to differ regarding drive - *striving* vs. *competing*.
Other	…	Much of the company and sales department tend to differ regarding factors such as vocabulary.

Example: Foster innovation

Situation

This example shows insight people can gain by using the checklist. Here, a corporation has a company-wide grassroots innovation program based in part on a new type of computer technology. Figure 42 indicates factors possibly affecting the company's prospects for entering into a corporate software license with a software provider.

Sometimes the parties reach an agreement. Sometimes they do not. The discussions in *Actionable meaning* and *Other* indicate that flexibility on the part of a provider can prove crucial.

In the figure,
- F> denotes perceived fact.
- A> denotes appraisal.

Figure 42 Interpreting an aspect of a company-wide innovation program

Endeavor >
A company improves its operations via a company-wide grassroots innovation program, based in part on a new type of information technology.
- Specifically, the company and a software provider attempt to do business with each other.

Themes	Typical Checklists	Instances
Useful proficiency	State Styles	F> The company and the provider realize that there are few precedents for the type of license they try to negotiate.
Actionable meaning	State Purposes	F> The company and the provider want the company to improve its operations via use of the provider's software. F> The company's approach to price focuses on the company's costs and the provider's profitability. F> The provider's approach to price originally focuses on gaining revenue. F> The provider's salesperson originally anticipates being compensated based on revenue generated. A> The company and the provider may (or may not) come to an agreement regarding this issue.
Innovative mindset	State Inventiveness	F> The company's approaches to its innovation needs and projects tend to be *ideate, instigate, invent,* and *implement*. F> The software provider's approaches to its products tend to be *ideate, instigate, invent,* and *innovate*. A> The two entities match regarding focusing on early-stage opportunities.
Competitive mindset	State Drive	F> The company's approaches to needs for innovation and to this program can be described as *competing*. F> The software provider's approach to developing its business can be characterized as *striving*. A> The two entities match as *diligent*.
Other	...	F> The company is sizable - in terms of revenue, staff, and procedure. F> The provider is small and flexible. A> The two entities may be matched (or mismatched) regarding abilities to work together.

Remarks

Without use of this checklist, negotiations evolve somewhat haphazardly. With use of the checklist, people can more readily guide likely deals to completion and more readily avoid trying to complete unlikely deals.

Chapter 15   State Inventiveness

Use the State Inventiveness checklist. Envision matches and mismatches between needs for innovation and proclivities of participants.

Figure 43 depicts the checklist.

Figure 43 State Inventiveness

	Endeavor	>	
	State Inventiveness		
Themes	Typical Activities		Instances
Reuses	Imitate		>
Synergies	Integrate		>
Uses	Implement		>
Products	Innovate		>
Prototypes	Invent		>
Ventures	Instigate		>
Concepts	Ideate		>
Passivity	Ignore		>
Opposition	Interfere		>

Too often, people miss opportunities to do the following (adequately well or at all).
- Determine activities or skills needed to effect desired innovation.
- Optimize or harmonize teams, activities, skills, attitudes, or proclivities regarding innovation.
- Characterize entities or activities based on their foci on various stages of innovation.
- Determine opportunities to change emphases regarding stages of innovation.

Consider using this checklist to help capture such opportunities. Figure 43 provides a guide. People can state instances in sentences paralleling the following or other prototypes.
- The endeavor needs [this activity].
- [This entity] does [this activity].
- [This entity] exhibits [this mindset].

In concept, do the following.
- Use the top row in the figure to describe an endeavor.
- Use the right column to record findings.
  - Consider that inventiveness might feature the following themes.
    - *Reuses / Imitate*: Implement (and integrate) parallel or competitive innovations.
    - *Synergies / Integrate*: Integrate implementations of innovations.
    - *Uses / Implement*: Derive benefit from an innovation or prototype.
    - *Products / Innovate*: Produce an innovation that users characterize as a product or service.

- *Prototypes / Invent*: Produce a useful prototype that could become a basis for a product or service.
- *Ventures / Instigate*: Launch a venture to develop, from a creative concept, at least a prototype.
- *Concepts / Ideate*: Create a concept that can be a basis for an innovation.
- *Passivity / Ignore*: Avoid a creative endeavor or an innovative product or service.
- *Opposition / Interfere*: Try to counter above-listed activities.
  - Describe instances.
    - Consider stating pros and cons of the instances.

Example: Interpret history

Endeavor

Envision or support possible innovations.

Situation

I participate in various efforts.

Actions based on thinking *inventiveness*

People propose innovations. Sometimes, people provide enough traction that innovation occurs. Sometimes, concepts for innovation go unused.

Results

The following innovations occur. For each, I note early-stage actions for which I have roles.
- Establish the Palos Verdes Estates Shoreline Preserve. Ideate.
- Develop software for scientific or business endeavors. Invent and implement.
- Develop software to aid software development. Ideate, instigate, invent, and implement.
- Develop an early multi-player computer game. Ideate, instigate, and invent.
- Develop other pioneering information technologies. Invent.
- Establish an international service program. Ideate.
- Establish the corporate software licensing practice. Invent, innovate, and implement.
- Establish, for an American political party's National Committee, a new line of business. Ideate.

For other efforts, I have later-stage roles.

Remarks

Instances illustrate State Inventiveness categories (Figure 43).
- (See the Results subsection, immediately above.)

Example: Hire salesperson

This example shows insight people can gain by using the checklist. Here, an organization tries to hire a salesperson. People can use the checklist to ideate. Figure 44 illustrates developing a checklist of topics for people to use in discussing with salesperson candidates the types of products or services a salesperson needs to sell to clients. People can decide the extent to discuss such topics.

State Inventiveness   63

Consider trying to use the checklist to think of other possible topics. Consider trying to add detail to various topics.

Figure 44 An application of State Inventiveness to hiring a salesperson

Endeavor > Hire a salesperson. • Specifically, conceive of types of products or services the salesperson may need to sell to a client.		
Themes	**Typical Activities**	**Instances**
Reuses	Imitate	Help the client develop products that imitate products of the client's competitors.
Synergies	Integrate	Help the client integrate its product lines. Help the client's customers integrate uses of the client's products with uses of other products.
Uses	Implement	Help the client's customers use the client's products.
Products	Innovate	Provide, for the client to resell, a line of products. Help the client develop a product from a prototype.
Prototypes	Invent	Develop a prototype for a product.
Ventures	Instigate	Provide leadership coaching.
Concepts	Ideate	Provide concepts for new products, services, or practices.
Passivity	Ignore	Help the client avoid doing research that is unlikely to produce a basis for appropriate products.
Opposition	Interfere	Help the client's customers decommission a product, or service. Help the client wind down a product line.

Example: Foster innovation

Situation

This example shows insight people can gain by using the checklist. Here, a corporation has a company-wide grassroots innovation program based in part on a new type of computer technology. Figure 45 indicates aspects and benefits of the program.

Figure 45 Interpreting an aspect of a company-wide innovation program

Endeavor > A company improves its operations via a company-wide grassroots innovation program, based in part on a new type of information technology. • Specifically, various entities participate in or otherwise benefit from the program.		
Themes	**Typical Activities**	**Instances**
Reuses	Imitate	Similar companies learn from the company's innovation program. Software customers (outside the company) and providers develop corporate software licenses.
Synergies	Integrate	The company's information technology department builds working relationships with groups and individuals with which the department previously had had little contact. Staff from various company regions form a council and coordinate developing and testing software applications.
Uses	Implement	Projects make more productive much company work.

Endeavor >		
A company improves its operations via a company-wide grassroots innovation program, based in part on a new type of information technology. • Specifically, various entities participate in or otherwise benefit from the program.		
Themes	**Typical Activities**	**Instances**
Products	Innovate	Some projects use products recently created by information-technology suppliers and make more productive some company operations that previously significantly used automation.
Prototypes	Invent	Projects invent new applications for the technology.
Ventures	Instigate	Project champions build teams and foster innovations.
Concepts	Ideate	Project champions create concepts for productivity improvements.
Passivity	Ignore	Some employees reportedly shun the new technology.
Opposition	Interfere	The company's software-licensing activities run counter to software providers' traditional business practices.

Remarks

Without use of this checklist, the list of such activities evolves haphazardly. With use of the checklist, people can systematically find and foster opportunities.

Chapter 16 State Drive

Use the State Drive checklist. Envision matches and mismatches between endeavor needs or cultures and participants' attitudes.

Figure 46 depicts the checklist.

Figure 46 State Drive

Endeavor	>

State Drive

Themes	Typical Attitudes	Instances
Leading / Diligent	Competing	>
Trailing / Diligent	Striving	>
Leading / Laidback	Coasting	>
Trailing / Laidback	Recollecting	>
Other	...	>

Too often, people miss opportunities to do the following (adequately well or at all).
- Characterize success and work culture of a society, coalition, organization, team, individual, endeavor, or activity.
- Influence success and work culture of a society, coalition, organization, team, individual, endeavor, or activity.

Consider using this checklist to help capture such opportunities. Figure 46 provides a guide. List *instances* of entities or activities. In concept, do the following.
- Use the top row in the figure to describe an endeavor.
- Use the right column to record findings.
  - Consider that the first four following items characterize four categories of success paired with attitude.
    - Leading / Diligent (*Competing*) ... refers to being relatively successful (compared to similar entities or activities) and being diligent at maintaining or enhancing relative success.
    - Trailing / Diligent (*Striving*) ... refers to being relatively unsuccessful (compared to similar entities or activities) and being diligent in trying to improve relative success.
    - Leading / Laidback (*Coasting*) ... refers to being relatively successful (compared to similar entities or activities) and being complacent about trying to maintain or enhance relative success.
    - Trailing / Laidback (*Striving*) ... refers to being relatively unsuccessful (compared to similar entities or activities) and being complacent about trying to improve relative success.
    - Other ... refers to other observations regarding success or attitudes.
  - Describe instances.
    - Consider stating pros and cons of the instances.

Example: Interpret history

Endeavor

Make recommendations to leaders of a political organization. In particular, review operations and suggest improvements.

Situation

Late twentieth century practices of an American political party's National Committee emphasize the following activities.
- Support some office-seeking candidate's campaigns.
- Help build some organizations, such as state parties.

Fundraising supports both types of activities.

During 2000, the organization runs a project to produce a report from the National Committee Chairman to the next cadre of leaders. I serve as the main consultant for the project.

Actions based on thinking *drive*

I recommend adding a grassroots line of business. I propose a theme of *winning hearts, minds, and participation of Americans*.

Results

In 2001, the National Committee forms a grassroots program and division. One part of the program attracts an online registration of at least 1.4 million *team leaders*.

Remarks

Instances illustrate State Drive categories (Figure 46).
- People might characterize as *coasting* the overall late twentieth century work of the National Committee. Much work features traditional goals and methods.
- People might characterize as *competing* some work using databases listing voters and much work by various people.
- People might characterize as *competing* the grassroots initiative. The National Committee enters a new line business.
- During the same period, people might characterize as *striving* or *recollecting* national-organization endeavors of American political parities other than the two largest parties.

Example: Hire salesperson

This example shows insight people can gain by using the checklist. Here, an organization tries to hire a salesperson. People can use the checklist to ideate. Figure 47 indicates possible generalizations regarding entities' behaviors. People can decide the extents to which a salesperson's actions need to cope with various entities' behaviors.

Consider trying to use the checklist to think of other possible instances. Consider trying to add detail to various instances.

Figure 47 An application of State Drive to hiring a salesperson

Endeavor >		
Hire a salesperson.		
• Specifically, prepare to select a preferred candidate.		
Themes	**Typical Attitudes**	**Instances**
Leading / Diligent	Competing	The organization's major competitors' general behavior
Trailing / Diligent	Striving	The organization's general behavior
Leading / Laidback	Coasting	Customer behavior regarding business in general
Trailing / Laidback	Recollecting	Customer behavior regarding the organization
Other	...	

Example: Foster innovation

Situation

This example shows insight people can gain by using the checklist. Here, a corporation has a company-wide grassroots innovation program based in part on a new type of computer technology. Figure 48 indicates general behaviors regarding completing deals to acquire a specific technology.

Figure 48 Interpreting an aspect of a company-wide innovation program

Endeavor >		
A company improves its operations via a company-wide grassroots innovation program, based in part on a new type of information technology.		
• Specifically, the company knows and can agree to major terms (quantity, price, and delivery schedule after contract signing) for possible deals with any one of several potential providers and the company is trying to close a deal with any of one of the potential providers.		
Themes	**Typical Attitudes**	**Instances**
Leading / Diligent	Competing	The company's behavior regarding productivity enhancement The company's behavior regarding trying to acquire technology from any one provider
Trailing / Diligent	Striving	A potential provider's salesperson's behavior regarding completing a deal
Leading / Laidback	Coasting	The potential provider's legal and other staff-function support for the provider's sales activity
Trailing / Laidback	Recollecting	The potential provider's abilities to develop teamwork between salespeople and sales-support staff functions
Other	...	

Remarks

Without use of this checklist, decisions about with which of several similar potential suppliers to vigorously attempt to close a deal evolve haphazardly. With use of the checklist, people can systematically allocate their attention to various suppliers.

Chapter 17   State Resources

Use the State Resources checklist. Determine capabilities needed so that endeavors succeed.

Figure 49 depicts the checklist.

Figure 49 State Resources

Endeavor	>

State Resources

Themes	Typical Needs	Resources and Practices
Skills	Perform work	>
Data	Use information	>
Entities	Meet desires for involvement	>
Reputations	Motivate constituents	>
Loyalties	Foster cohesiveness	>
Funds	Acquire services	>
Infrastructure	Support work	>
Freedom	Have time	>
Other	...	>

Too often, people miss opportunities to do the following (adequately well or at all).
- Determine resources and practices associated with an endeavor.
  - Resources can include skills, individuals, data, systems, funds, or other resources.
- Determine resources and practices that should - or should not - be associated with an endeavor.
- Gather or grow resources and practices appropriate for an endeavor.
- Ensure resources and practices have appropriate skills and support.

Consider using this checklist to help capture such opportunities. Figure 49 provides a guide. In concept, do the following.
- Use the top row in the figure to describe an endeavor.
- Use the right column to record findings.
  - Consider that resources and practices might feature the following themes.
    - *Skills* might include leadership, subject matter abilities (for example, in marketing, finance, or engineering), fluency in a language, proficiency with a system or method, and so forth.
    - *Data* might include data in people's minds, on paper, in information systems, and so forth.
    - *Entities* might include a resource or combination of resources. An entity might desire or be expected to participate in an endeavor.
    - *Reputations* might depend on pairs of entities, with one entity having an opinion about the other entity. Examples of reputations might include ethical, trustworthy, visionary, deliberate, supportive, aggressive, and so forth.

- *Loyalties* might be to entities or principles generally harmonious with, generally hostile to, or so forth aspects of an endeavor.
- *Funds* might be available to acquire products, services, ownership in companies, and so forth.
- *Infrastructure* might include communications systems, information processing systems, food, energy supplies, office space, and means of transportation.
- *Freedom* might include time or times to devote to the endeavor.
- *Other* might include, for example, brochures.
- Describe resources and practices.
    - Consider stating pros and cons of the resources and practices.

Example: Interpret history

Endeavor

A startup company tries to supply a customer with an information system.

Situation

The customer wants to improve services to its clients. The customer wants to reduce the size of the customer's clerical staff.

The startup needs to develop new types of hardware and software. The startup's technology team assumes the system will strain the capabilities of relevant computers. The team strives to remain small and to develop useful software on time. The team wants to streamline software development.

Actions based on thinking *resources*

The team builds software-development tools.

Results

The customer reduces its *average elapsed time per case* from eight weeks to two weeks. The startup pioneers the *automated document library*.

Reuses

The startup's parent company creates a line of business - providing systems that store and present images. The software-development tools evolve into yet another line of business.

Remarks

Resources and practices illustrate State Resources categories (Figure 49).
- The team needs *skills* and computing *infrastructure* sufficient to build the tools.
- Given limitations imposed by the main computer system (*infrastructure*), developing and deploying user-perceived flawless software might be impossible (*time*) or overly expensive (*funds*) without standardizing key software-development processes.
- The startup and its parent want to maintain and enhance their *reputations* for satisfying customers' needs and pioneering useful technologies.

State Resources

Example: Hire salesperson

This example shows insight people can gain by using the checklist. Here, an organization tries to hire a salesperson. People can use the checklist to ideate. Figure 50 indicates some resources and practices the organization's people may want to feature when recruiting candidates. To the extent such resources and practices are lacking, candidates may decide not to accept job offers. Possibly, people should be prepared to discuss achievements, plans, and synergies related to the resources and practices. People can decide the extent to discuss such resources and practices.

Consider trying to use the checklist to think of other possible resources and practices. Consider trying to add detail to various resources and practices.

Figure 50 An application of State Resources to hiring a salesperson

Endeavor >		
Hire a salesperson.		
• Specifically, discuss the organization's resources and practices. Thereby, help a salesperson decide whether to accept an offer and then, if appropriate, help the salesperson to get started working.		
Themes	**Typical Needs**	**Resources and Practices**
Skills	Perform work	Existing sales practices Support for sales work from marketing, legal, technical, and customer-service staff Support for a new hire's getting started
Data	Use information	Leads Intelligence regarding marketplaces and customers
Entities	Meet desires for involvement	Customers that might want to make new purchases Boss, colleagues, and support staff Information systems
Reputations	Motivate constituents	Reputations of the organization, its products and services, and its sales practices
Loyalties	Foster cohesiveness	Efforts, by the organization, on behalf of *the public interest*
Funds	Acquire services	Compensation package - salary and benefits Budget that supports sales work
Infrastructure	Support work	Means of transportation to customer sites
Freedom	Have time	The organization's practices for various types of sales work and related work
Other	…	Marketing materials

Example: Foster innovation

Situation

This example shows insight people can gain by using the checklist. Here, a corporation has a company-wide grassroots innovation program based in part on a new type of computer technology. Figure 51 indicates aspects of building corporate and personal resources. In the figure,
- A> denotes actual aspects of the program.
- N> denotes aspects of traditional practice that the program deemphasizes.

Figure 51 Interpreting an aspect of a company-wide innovation program

Endeavor >		
A company improves its operations via a company-wide grassroots innovation program, based in part on a new type of information technology. • Specifically, the program helps develop company resources.		
Themes	**Typical Needs**	**Resources and Practices**
Skills	Perform work	A> People's learning how to use information technology is based on on-the-job learning. N> People's education features attending classes.
Data	Use information	A> People develop uses for the new technology that improve the use of centralized data, such as sales-related, customer-service, and financial information. N> Uses of new technologies jeopardize the quality or value of the data stored in traditional systems.
Entities	Meet desires for involvement	A> Organizations and individuals choose their own degrees of involvement. The program emphasizes grassroots, voluntary participation. N> An information technology group leads projects.
Reputations	Motivate constituents	A> The program-catalyzing group markets the success of project champions and their projects. N> New projects shun publicity in fear of becoming regulated by an information technology department.
Loyalties	Foster cohesiveness	A> Projects align with company goals and needs. N> Projects risk fostering undue isolation among work-improvement coalitions and efforts.
Funds	Acquire services	A> The program avoids processes to review planned capital expenditures, in part because projects are approved by company officers. N> Various organizations - beyond and in the information-technology department - scramble to find funds to acquire standard types of technology.
Infrastructure	Support work	A> The company deploys standard software for doing widespread types of work. N> Use of disparate software makes sharing data and methods unnecessarily difficult.
Freedom	Have time	A> Productivity enhancements free people's time and permit the people to address other work. N> Developing computer applications requires work by application-development experts.
Other	…	

Remarks

Without use of this checklist, the list of such resources and practices evolves haphazardly. With use of the checklist, people can systematically strengthen company operations and improve people's projects, skills, and potential for having satisfying careers.

Part 3 Learn More

Too often, efforts fall short. Too often, people may think - at least unconsciously - some of the following thoughts about insight.
- "It's about people we know, not people we could know."
- "It's about today, not tomorrow."
- "It's about here, not everywhere."
- "It's about being, not thriving."
- "It's about inputs, not outcomes."
- "It's about busyness, not business."
- "It's about being manipulative, not being compelling."
- "It's about belief, not evidence."
- "It's about win-lose, not win-win."
- "It's about feeling good, not doing good."
- "It's about what is, not what could be."
- "It's about getting by, not getting ahead."
- "It's about technology, not people."

This book provides ways to avoid or minimize negative results. This book provides ways to create or enhance positive results.

This part of the book provides the following opportunities.
- Use the Foster Win-Win technique. Help clients and providers optimize results for each other.
- Use Detail Opportunities information. Gain insight about uses for and origins of Direct Outcomes.
- Use the Describe Capabilities technique. Develop themes for marketing entities' services.
- Use Teach Methods techniques. Help people learn and use work methods and work-improvement methods.
- Use the Create Metrics technique. Help people create and use metrics.
- Use Create Methods techniques. Help people create, extend, integrate, and select methods and checklists.
- Learn about this book's author, Dr. Thomas J. Buckholtz.
- Learn about this book's parts, chapters, chapter summaries, and figures.

Chapter 18   Foster Win-Win

Use the Foster Win-Win technique. Help clients and providers optimize results for each other.

Figure 37 depicts the State Teamwork checklist.

Too often, people miss opportunities to do the following (adequately well or at all).
- Become a better provider.
    - Become better at working with clients or potential clients.
    - Improve products or services.
    - Improve use of support from clients.
- Become a better client.
    - Become better at working with providers or potential providers.
    - Improve use of products or services.
    - Improve use of support from providers.
- Help a client and a provider improve their support for each other.
- Gain effectiveness at facilitating relationships between clients and providers.

Much work involves client-provider relationships. People may be able to benefit from such opportunities many times per day.

Consider using the State Teamwork checklist (Figure 37) to help capture such opportunities. Consider using the column labeled *Entity 1* for the client. Consider using the column labeled *Entity 2* for the provider.

Example: Improve a provider's products and services

People can consider doing the following to improve a provider's products and services.

Situation

Think of an instance - preferably real but, if not, hypothetical - of a client, a provider, and their relationship.

The State Teamwork checklist (Figure 37) calls attention to *outcomes the client wants* and *reuses the client wants*. The State Progress checklist provides a basis for developing a client-centric plan.
- The client seeks to do the following.
    - Achieve and measure outcomes (as symbolized by the Outcomes category in State Progress).
    - Do so appropriately (via activities associated with subsequent State Progress categories).
    - Reuse aspects of the outcomes and activities (as symbolized by the Reuses category).
- The provider's support might …
    - Include services by the provider.
    - Include services the client derives from products from the provider.
    - Contribute to the client's success regarding any of the State Progress categories.
- The State Progress categories Reuses through Resources provide opportunities to envision activities - by or on behalf of the client - that help the client achieve outcomes (or reuses).

Actions

Associate the client's outcomes with the Outcomes category in the State Progress checklist.

Develop a plan for what the client needs to ensure happens so that the outcomes (and reuses) occur.
- Think of activities corresponding to the categories in the checklist.
  - Figure 52 suggests descriptions and placements for some types of activities.
- Feel free to add to the suggestions.
  - Feel free to add activities.
    - Feel free to add activities that are more specific than ones the figure lists.
  - If people suggest more than one category for an activity, feel free to put the activity in any one or more such categories.

Figure 52 Needs of a client's endeavor

Endeavor >	
A client thrives, in part based on services by a provider or by products from the provider.	
Themes	**Types of Client Activities**
Reuses	Provide testimonials about the services or provider. Use the services, beyond the endeavor. Acquire other services from the provider.
Outcomes	Recognize its business outcomes and the extent to which the services contributed. Attribute value to the outcomes and services.
Actions	Conduct its business. Within that business, receive and use the services. Close a deal to acquire the services.
Plans	Choose a combination of scenarios for conducting its business. Decide to what extent to try to acquire the services.
Scenarios	Develop scenarios for conducting its business. Include, in scenarios, varying degrees of use of the provider's or similar services.
Assumptions	Perceive information and assumptions about its business and suppliers. Note possible uses of services from and possible relationships with providers.
Interactions	Ensure its resources work together appropriately - with themselves and with its providers.
Motivations	Find and understand factors that motivate resources to participate - in the overall endeavor and with respect to providers and the provider.
Resources	Involve appropriate resources (people, organizations, data, information systems, other equipment, buildings, funds, and so forth). Identify inappropriate ones.

By now, people likely can identify opportunities for the provider's improving the value it contributes toward the client's achieving outcomes (and reuses). Perhaps some of the opportunities are similar to the *types of provider activities* listed in Figure 53. For example, the Interactions activities may point to opportunities to improve work by or coordination between provider components such as a salesperson, a product-design team, or service-department functions.

Figure 53 Activities for a provider

Endeavor >	
A client thrives, in part based on services by a provider or by products from the provider.	
Themes	**Types of Provider Activities**
Reuses	Solicit and broadcast testimonials. Encourage the client to propagate testimonials, at least within the client. Suggest client uses for the services, beyond the endeavor.
Outcomes	Provide the client methods for recognizing and measuring its business outcomes and the extent to which the services contributed.

Endeavor >	
A client thrives, in part based on services by a provider or by products from the provider.	
Themes	**Types of Provider Activities**
Actions	Provide support for client's use of the services. Use usage information to improve the services. Make it easy to close a deal for the client to acquire the services.
Plans	Help the client estimate the desirability of pursuing various scenarios, including varied usage of the provider's services.
Scenarios	Help the client develop scenarios for conducting its business, including varying degrees of use of the provider's or similar services.
Assumptions	Learn about the client. Provide information about the provider's business, possible client uses of the provider's services, and possible client-provider relationships.
Interactions	Ensure its resources work together appropriately - with themselves and with the client.
Motivations	Find and understand factors that motivate client or provider resources to participate - in the overall endeavor and with respect to the client.
Resources	Involve appropriate resources (people, organizations, data, information systems, other equipment, buildings, funds, and so forth). Identify inappropriate ones.

Next steps can include the following.
- People prioritize the provider's opportunities.
- The provider decides the extent to try to capture such opportunities.

Results

People create a roadmap for improving the provider's service to the client.

Reuses

The provider can use the roadmap to guide evolution of its products and services. The provider can use Direct Outcomes to do the following.
- Reprioritize service-improvement projects.
- Develop marketing themes regarding the provider's services.
- Personalize marketing messages, based on audiences (even within a single client).

Remarks

This example features using State Progress to envision a provider's opportunities to improve its products for and services to clients.

Consider using the example to determine how a client can better serve needs of a provider. Use the example, with the two roles exchanged.

Chapter 19 Detail Opportunities

Use Detail Opportunities information. Gain insight about uses for and origins of Direct Outcomes.

Figure 6 lists Direct Outcomes checklists.

Too often, people miss opportunities to do the following (adequately well or at all).
- Pinpoint issues, problems, and opportunities more clearly and more usefully than people might otherwise do.
- Discover possibilities people might otherwise overlook.
  - Such possibilities can include goals, producible products, product features, service improvements, marketing messages, reusable work, work simplifications, allies, and so forth.
- Perform work more successfully than people might otherwise do.
- Gain capability and flexibility to innovate - or to relax.

Specifically, people miss opportunities to do the following (adequately well or at all).
- Generate useful perspective.
  - Frame issues clearly.
  - Pinpoint problems and identify solutions.
  - Create and capture opportunities.
- Set appropriate work scope and working environment.
  - Focus on important matters.
  - Harmonize broad-endeavor goals and narrower-activity goals and incentives.
  - Optimize the use and reuse of resources.
  - Integrate appropriately work, innovation, and learning.
  - Balance spontaneity and routine.
  - Encourage people to use mutually useful frameworks and vocabularies for working together.
  - Apply (systematically) rigorous qualitative checklists to improve doing any or all of the above.
- Help people determine and communicate the following.
  - People need to do [this].
  - People need to do such [this well].
  - People can do such [this way].
  - [These people] should do such.
  - Dong such can have [this impact].
- Perform vital work.
  - Measure what is.
  - Anticipate what could be.
  - Make and implement decisions.
  - Produce what should be.
  - Measure results achieved.
  - Reuse what people achieve and learn.
- Study, create, augment, select, integrate, and use methods and checklists.
  - Study methods (possibly including Direct Outcomes).
  - Build methods. Evolve or augment existing methods.
  - Use or benefit from a repertoire of methods. Measure the usage of methods.
  - Teach methods.

Consider using Direct Outcomes checklists to help capture such opportunities.

Examples: Use State Styles to address issues, problems, and opportunities

The following examples illustrate uses of State Styles to frame an issue, pinpoint a problem, and spot an opportunity.
- Frame an issue.
  - "To what extent does our work culture impact our success?"
    - Consider that a dimension of work culture features styles characterizing work.
    - Use State Styles to analyze work activities and culture and to envision future alternative work behaviors.
    - Evaluate the desirability of trying to change work styles.
- Pinpoint a problem.
  - "Given that our competitors produce products of similar quality to our products but via lower-cost methods, which of our processes should we improve?"
    - Consider that - on the State Styles scale - performing an activity at closer to Effortless style (than the style characterizing current work) may lower costs.
    - Analyze, to the extent appropriate, competitors' production activities. Use State Styles as a metric.
    - Evaluate activities for the potential to move working styles up on the State Styles scale.
- Spot an opportunity.
  - "Our employees have suggested numerous possible improvements for our processes. Which of the suggested improvements should we implement?"
    - Use work styles and their situation-specific implications to provide some criteria for evaluating the relative merits of the suggestions.
    - Consider using State Styles to help evaluate the suitability of work-improvement techniques.

Example: Evolve Direct Outcomes

Situation
People need useful, straightforward ways to think about and influence endeavors.

Actions
I anticipate that people can benefit from using widely applicable checklists. I realize I have such checklists to offer. I develop the Direct Outcomes program.

Results
Direct Outcomes currently includes eleven checklists.

Remarks
In engineering, finance, and other specialties, people use quantitative models and other methods to streamline and improve work. Science, mathematics, or other fundamentals may underlie such methods.

Qualitative rigorous methods underlie key Direct Outcomes checklists. People can use Direct Outcomes checklists to bring new proficiency to not-fully-quantized work.

I use Direct Outcomes to help me evolve and offer Direct Outcomes checklists.

Detail Opportunities

Examples: Declare potential benefits of using Direct Outcomes

The following statements indicate potential benefits of using Direct Outcomes. (In some statements, I changed the names of checklists to reflect [current terminology]. In one statement, I inserted {i.e., [current terminology]}. In one statement, I noted (sic).)

- A Fortune 50 telecommunications company director estimated a potential for $2 million in annual revenue gains by using results from doing succession planning, based on Direct Outcomes, for the director's own job. Regarding succession planning itself, the director called the Direct-Outcomes-based succession-planning findings more accurate, more useful, and more defensible than results obtained a month earlier via the company's traditional method.
    - (This statement summarizes remarks during a workshop.)
- A Direct Outcomes workshop provides participants with practical and easy-to-understand techniques for assessing an organization's performance and for executing business strategies.
    - Walter Kruz, Founder, Recova Research and Adjunct Professor, Lincoln University
- Dr. Buckholtz has developed an easy-to-use model for organizational improvement. It is quickly implemented and can be used in a variety of situations. I recommend the [State Progress checklist] to anyone who needs a simple guide for organized decision making and effective communication.
    - Lin Marelick, Dean of Workforce Development, Mission College
- Direct Outcomes is a meta-level flexible tool kit for clarifying issues and accomplishing results throughout a wide range of business and personal situations. Tom Buckholtz is providing tools through which people can function and innovate at his level - from big-picture thinking through focused specifics. Direct Outcomes is truly useful for all seasons.
    - Howard Lieberman, Chairman / CEO, Silicon Valley Innovation Institute
- To create, clarify and capture opportunities are the challenges we continually face in any endeavor. Direct Outcomes presents a cogent and practical framework to tease out what we can, should and must do. The tremendous utility of Direct Outcomes is that you may begin at where you are. As you gather more information / understanding the framework leads you to integrated solutions. As a project line manager and consultant I am always looking for a practical tool set. Direct Outcomes is that tool set of broad applicability that yields clear, specific and actionable direction.
    - John Pettigrew, Principal, Real Change Consultancy
- Dr Buckholtz's 'Direct Outcomes' is a gem of practical frameworks for business decision making. It tackles the seemingly mundane notions of style, services, impact, needs, methods, and outcomes while wrapping them into a robust pragmatic framework to help analyze and direct management decisions for remarkably impressive measurable results. Direct Outcomes has broad applicability helping my IT consulting practice in areas as diverse as streamlining IT business continuity processes to designing and implementing value-rich design patterns in systems and software. ... Over time, ... the methodology becomes each practitioner's inimitable, native, but fundamental modus operandi.
    - Alexander Factor, Principal, Factor Consulting
- At last, a pragmatic approach to organizational and individual improvement - as deep in practical advice as it is comprehensive in scope. An approach that any executive or professional can relate to and implement quickly. In his [Direct Outcomes] technique, Dr. Buckholtz has captured the essential factors for effecting successful and substantial enterprise and personal effectiveness improvements.
    - Joe Feliu, Vice President, NeoDimensions, Inc; former VP Operations/CIO, Visto Corp and AllAdvantage.com; Adjunct Instructor University of San Francisco and Anderson School of Management/UCLA

- The [State Progress] technique provides a valuable tool for determining the essential details needed to achieve a business objective.
    - Roberta Moore, CEO, Revenue Optimization Council; Founder, Qualitative Marketing
- The application of Direct Outcomes' philosophy and tactics has the potential to be as important to the first half of the 21st Century as was the application of statistics and game theory to marketing and business strategy during the fourth quarter of the 20th Century. Will it became a core competency taught in Business School like the math tools above? I don't know; but I do know that smart, progressive businesses that adopt the Direct Outcomes structural view will have significant strategic and operation advantage over their competitors.
    - Harrison Rose; Founder and Vice President Business Development, Marketing, and Sales; Nisvara, Inc.
- The [State Progress] technique is a must-implement tool for Business Executives - indeed, anyone - focused on attaining results through pragmatic Decision Making and Effective Communication.
    - Ken Danchi, President & CEO, Plassmosoft Communications, Ghana
- The [State Progress] and [State Styles] techniques provide as important a conceptual breakthrough for enhancing business success as have Relativity and Quantum Mechanics for keeping physics viable. Fortunately, unlike Relativity or Quantum Theory, almost any person, group, or enterprise can benefit quickly and significantly from Value {i.e., Progress} and Maturity {i.e., Styles}.
    - Ron Fredericks, President and CEO, Embedded Components, Inc.
- I think that this [Direct Outcomes] course would work well for individuals that a company is 'watching' for promotion. It gives them an intellectual tool that is easily put into conventional practice.
    - A workshop participant
- Direct Outcomes provides an improved performance review metric … The [State Styles] scale gives the employee non-arbitrary, achievable and concrete performance targets that focus on improvement of the quality of work processes.
    - A student in a leadership and innovation class
- These [Direct Outcomes checklists] are very useful for almost all jobs … The concept of basically planning on how to affect (sic) change is a very good one. It's not just "make a good top-down plan," but rather "make a plan, thinking about how to bring in other constituents, and achieve synergy."
    - A student in a leadership and innovation class
- Each [Direct Outcomes checklist] can be used in a way that provides insight into dimensions of the customer's perspective and needs.
    - A student in a leadership and innovation class

Chapter 20 Describe Capabilities

Use the Describe Capabilities technique. Develop themes for marketing entities' services.

Figure 54 depicts the technique.

Figure 54 Describe Capabilities

Endeavor >			
Bases for Concepts for Typical Actions	**Typical Actions**	**Instances**	**Themes**
>	>	>	>
>	>	>	>
>	>	>	>
>	>	>	>
>	>	>	>

Too often, people miss opportunities to do the following (adequately well or at all).
- Develop a list of capabilities of an organization or individual.
- Use a list of capabilities to develop themes for brochures, presentations, resumes, or other marketing materials.

Consider using this technique to help capture such opportunities. Figure 54 provides a guide. Identify capabilities of an entity. Develop marketing themes. (The following section, *Example: Add key experience and skills to a resume*, provides an example. After that section, Figure 55 provides examples of the leftmost two Figure 54 columns.) In concept, do the following.
- Use the top row in the figure to describe an endeavor.
- Use the leftmost column to name *bases for concepts for typical actions*.
  - An *action* is an activity that the entity to be marketed performed, performs, or can perform.
  - A *basis for concepts* is a model (or other basis) people can use to can envision *actions*.
  - People can use Direct Outcomes checklists and other methods as *bases*.
- Use the second column to describe *typical actions*.
  - People can determine such actions from categories associated with Direct Outcomes checklists.
  - People can determine such actions from facets of other methods.
  - People can determine actions without associating the actions with a *basis*.
- Use the third column record *instances* or summarizes of instances.
  - An *instance* is an example of the entity to be marketed performing (or helping other entities perform) a *typical action*.
  - People can base *instances* on the following premises.
    - The entity performs a *typical action*.
    - The entity helps [this other entity] perform a *typical action*.
    - The entity helps [this other entity] help [this yet other entity] perform a *typical action*.
  - For an *instance*, the following statements pertain.
    - People can base the instance on past work or future potential.
    - People can record a situation, some actions, and results.
  - For summarizing similar *instances*, the following pertain.
    - People can generalize specific situations to more-general circumstances, specific actions to more-general actions, and specific results to more-general results.

- People can consider the extents to which audiences for marketing statements may find appealing either type - specific or general - of statement.
- Use the right column to summarize marketing themes people develop based on *instances*.

Example: Add key experience and skills to a resume

This example illustrates using the Describe Capabilities technique to help develop a resume.

The following pertain.
- *Endeavor*: A person writes a resume to support the person's seeking a higher-level job than the person holds.
- A *basis for concepts for typical actions*: The *Other Synergies* category of the State Synergies checklist.
- A *typical action*: Help [this endeavor or entity] work with [this endeavor or entity].
  - (See, in Figure 55 below, the *typical actions* rows devoted to State Synergies as a *basis for concepts for typical actions*.)
- *Instances*: The person helps people negotiate and achieve productive working relationships.
- *Themes*:
  - Negotiation
  - Mediation

The person does the following.
- Recognize the person's negotiating and mediation successes.
- Realize that the higher-level job requires negotiating and mediation skills.
- Add negotiation and mediation skills and successes to a resume that otherwise would not mention such.

Example: Use Direct Outcomes to determine typical actions

Figure 55 shows results of using Direct Outcomes checklists to determine *typical actions*.
- Rows in the figure provide interpretations of the respective categories of the respective Direct Outcomes checklists.
  - People can make and use other interpretations.
- Regarding using the figure,
  - People can treat *[this ...]* and *[these ...]* phrases as suggesting people specify the following.
    - Actual names or descriptions of entities (or results, plans, or so forth)
    - Generic classes of entities (or results, plans, or so forth)
  - People can add or change *typical actions* items (with or without specifying *bases for concepts*).

Figure 55 From Direct Outcomes checklists to some typical actions

Bases for Concepts for Typical Actions	Typical Actions
State Synergies	Help [this customer] achieve [this result].
State Synergies	Help [this partner or colleague] achieve [this result].
State Synergies	Help [this entity] work with [this provider].
State Synergies	Evolve [this relationship or skill] over time.
State Synergies	Help [this endeavor or entity] work with [this endeavor or entity].
State Impact	Summarize [these findings].
State Impact	Make [this decision].

Describe Capabilities 85

Bases for Concepts for Typical Actions	Typical Actions
State Impact	Find [this significant point] in [this information].
State Impact	Evaluate [these differences] between [these results, services, products, skills, or so forth].
State Impact	Choose [this metric] to measure [this result, service, product, skill, or so forth].
State Impact	Find [these differences] between [these results, services, products, skills, or so forth].
State Impact	Find [these similarities or this common ground] regarding [these issues, results, services, products, skills, or so forth].
State Impact	Develop [these alternative scenarios] for [this endeavor].
State Impact	Frame context for [this situation].
State Progress	Foster [this reuse] of [this product or skill].
State Progress	Recognize [this outcome] from [this endeavor].
State Progress	Perform [this action].
State Progress	Choose [this plan] for achieving [this result] or performing [this action].
State Progress	Envision [this scenario] for [this endeavor].
State Progress	Guide the making of [this assumption] or using of [this information] in support of making [this decision].
State Progress	Guide [this interaction] between [this entity] and [this entity].
State Progress	Motivate [this person or organization] to take [this action].
State Progress	Involve [this resource] in [this endeavor].
State Styles	Make it unnecessary to do [this work].
State Styles	Integrate [these elements of work].
State Styles	Make [this work] more routine.
State Styles	Experiment with or compare [these ways] of doing [this work].
State Styles	Generate [this result] via [this unstructured work].
State Styles	Defer when appropriate [this work].
State Purposes	Enhance [this facet] of [this person's] life or of the *fabric of society*.
State Purposes	Satisfy or effect [this principle, standard, agenda, or goal].
State Purposes	Provide [this resource, method, or knowledge].
State Purposes	Help [this person] have [this experience or relationship].
State Purposes	Optimize risk taking [in this situation] or exposure to [this risk].
State Purposes	Gain [this goal, purpose, or sense of direction].
State Purposes	Ally with or create [this entity, relationship, or activity].
State Purposes	Deploy, gain, or create [this resource, method, skill, or knowledge].
State Purposes	Enhance [this reputation], as seen by [this entity].
State Purposes	Attain [this certification or other recognition].
State Purposes	Maintain or enhance [this type - for example, medical or financial - of wellness].
State Purposes	Other (Specify.):
State Assumptions	Determine the sufficiency for [this use] of [this assumption or information].
State Assumptions	Derive [this insight].
State Assumptions	Evaluate the usefulness of [this information].
State Assumptions	Evaluate the intrinsic quality of [this information].
State Assumptions	Involve [this data] in [this work].
State Assumptions	Specify or use [this metadata].
State Teamwork	Name or describe [this entity].
State Teamwork	Recognize that [this entity] wants [this outcome] to occur.

Bases for Concepts for Typical Actions	Typical Actions
State Teamwork	Recognize that [this entity] wants [this reuse of progress] to occur.
State Teamwork	Recognize that [these entities] support each other via [this activity].
State Teamwork	Recognize that [this entity] performs [this function].
State Teamwork	Recognize that [this entity] exhibits [this persona].
State Teamwork	Recognize that [this person] performs [this work].
State Tendencies	Determine styles with which [this entity] does [this activity].
State Tendencies	Determine that [this entity] pursues [this purpose].
State Tendencies	Determine that [this entity] exhibits [this behavior] regarding innovation.
State Tendencies	Determine that [this entity] exhibits [this competitive mindset].
State Tendencies	Other (Specify.):
State Inventiveness	Imitate [this action or product].
State Inventiveness	Integrate [these actions or products].
State Inventiveness	Implement [this action or product].
State Inventiveness	Innovate, thereby producing [this action or product].
State Inventiveness	Invent prototypes for [this action or product].
State Inventiveness	Instigate [this endeavor or action].
State Inventiveness	Create [this concept].
State Inventiveness	Ignore [this endeavor].
State Inventiveness	Interfere with or wind down [this endeavor].
State Drive	Exhibit [this diligent behavior] while having [this leading position].
State Drive	Exhibit [this diligent behavior] while having [this trailing position].
State Drive	Exhibit [this laidback behavior] while having [this leading position].
State Drive	Exhibit [this laidback behavior] while having [this trailing position].
State Drive	Other (Specify.):
State Resources	Exhibit [this skill].
State Resources	Have [this information].
State Resources	Deal with [this entity's desires] regarding involvement in [this endeavor].
State Resources	Motivate [this constituent] to take [this action].
State Resources	Foster loyalty from [this entity] to [this cause or entity].
State Resources	Acquire or use [these funds] to accomplish [this end].
State Resources	Deploy [this element of infrastructure] to help achieve [this end].
State Resources	Have time to perform [this action].
State Resources	Other (Specify):
	[Other]

Perspective

People can use the Describe Capabilities technique to envision services entities need.

Chapter 21   Teach Methods

Use Teach Methods techniques. Help people learn and use work methods and work-improvement methods.

The Track Utilization technique (depicted in Figure 18) provides a measuring technique. The State Progress checklist (Figure 25) provides a basis for plans and actions.

Too often, people miss opportunities to do the following (adequately well or at all).
- Participate in programs that help learners do the following.
  - Develop and maintain motivations to learn and use methods.
  - Maintain consciousness about the potential for learning, using, benefitting from, and teaching the methods.
  - Use the methods.
  - Measure learners' progress.
- Help learners teach themselves.
- Identify activities that learners can perform to learn methods.
- Provide teachers and coaches with menus of activities for learners. Thereby, help teachers and coaches develop and deliver learning programs as varied as the following.
  - An individual learner learns, uses, benefits from, and teaches methods.
  - An enterprise trains employees to provide workshops and coaching through which people can learn methods. Organizations and individuals adopt and benefit sustainably from methods taught.

Consider using the Track Utilization technique and the State Progress checklist to help capture such opportunities. Figure 18 and Figure 25 provide a guide. In concept, do the following.
- Use the top row in the figures to describe an endeavor.
  - Include in the description the following.
    - People who should learn
    - Methods people should learn
    - Expectations about the extent to which people's capabilities should develop
- Use the right column in Figure 25 to record planned or actual learner activities.
- Use the right column in Figure 18 to record learners' utilization of the methods.

Example: Develop lists of activities for learners

This example shows how people can develop lists of activities for learners of methods.

People can use the following steps.
- Envision needs of learners (individuals, teams, or organizations) and people with whom learners interact.
- Use State Progress to determine activities learners might perform.
  - For example, modify and add to the list of activities in the right column of Figure 56.
- Tailor lists and activities to specific learners and circumstances.

Figure 56 Learn and benefit from methods

Endeavor >	
Learn and benefit from methods (possibly including Direct Outcomes).	
Themes	**Types of Learner's Activities**
Reuses	Encourage people to use results and lessons-learned from the learner's use of methods. • Encourage such people to do (as learners) activities listed in this column. Show people how the learner uses and benefits from methods. Encourage people to pursue appropriate issues, problems, and opportunities, based on needs to address such issues and problems, advantages of pursuing such opportunities, and a better-than-traditional repertoire of methods. Develop new methods that augment or integrate traditional methods.
Outcomes	Document results the learner achieves via methods. Measure benefits the learner achieves for other people or for the learner - in general and because of using specific methods.
Actions	Deploy methods while conducting the learner's life and business activities. Use methods-usage plans.
Plans	Integrate methods-usage plans into broader plans. Develop methods-usage plans.
Scenarios	Build scenarios for deploying methods for the following work. • Work the learner anticipates • Work the learner recalls from the past • Work the learner hypothesizes
Assumptions	Determine assumptions about the applicability of various methods to the following work. • Work the learner anticipates • Work the learner recalls from the past • Work the learner hypothesizes Determine work the learner needs to do and assumptions that likely apply to the work.
Interactions	Work with other people, in part based on knowledge of those people's methods.
Motivations	Determine the learner's attitudes and motivations (practical and emotional) regarding using methods.
Resources	Learn of the existence and characteristics of methods by doing, for example, the following. • Make on-the-job usage of methods. • Work with colleagues or coaches who discuss or use methods. • Read books. • Participate in formal programs, such as workshops. • Extrapolate methods from observations about patterns pertaining to work.

Chapter 22   Create Metrics

Use the Create Metrics technique. Help people create and use metrics.

Figure 57 depicts the technique.

Figure 57   Create Metrics

Endeavor >						
Facets being Measured	Themes for Evaluations	Themes for Metrics	Bases for Categories	Categories for Topics	Topics for Evaluation	Findings
>	>	>	>	>	>	>
>	>	>	>	>	>	>
>	>	>	>	>	>	>
>	>	>	>	>	>	>
>	>	>	>	>	>	>

Too often, people miss opportunities to do the following (adequately well or at all).
- Use metrics.
- Create or select apt metrics.
- Avoid using conflicting metrics.
- Augment or avoid nebulous metrics.
    - For example, substitute a more-meaningful metric for *outstanding, excellent, good …*
- Augment or avoid numeric results based on qualitative ratings.
    - For example, augment *5 = very much, 4 = somewhat …*
- Focus enough on both outcomes and inputs.
- Make qualitative metrics more situation-specific.

Consider using this technique to help capture such opportunities. Figure 57 provides a guide. (The following section, *Example: Evaluate attitudes toward work*, provides an example. Then, the section, *Example: Evaluate marketing themes*, provides another example. After that section, Figure 58 provides examples of the leftmost four Figure 57 columns.) In concept, do the following.
- Use the top row in the figure to describe an endeavor.
- Use the left column to describe endeavor *facets being measured*.
- Use the second column to describe *themes for evaluations* of the facets.
- Use the third column to describe *themes for metrics*.
- Use the fourth column to list *bases for categories*.
    - Anticipate using the bases to determine categories for the following.
        - Determining and cataloging *topics for evaluation*.
        - Summarizing *findings* relevant to possibly related topics.
- Use the fifth column to list *categories for topics* to evaluate.
- Use the sixth column to list *topics for evaluation*.
- Use the right column to record measurements and other *findings* about *facets*.

Example: Evaluate attitudes toward work

This example shows how people can use the Create Metrics technique to help evaluate people's attitudes regarding work comprising an endeavor.

Situation

The following pertain.
- *Facet being measured*: Attitudes (toward the endeavor)
- *Theme for evaluations*: Attitudes regarding types of work
- *Themes for metrics*: Likes and dislikes
- *Bases for categories*: State Progress and State Style
- *Categories for topics*: One of more of the following
  - All or some of the nine State Progress categories
    - These categories focus on kinds of work people do.
  - All or some of the six State Styles categories
    - For example, the last four State Styles categories (Procedural through Nil)
    - These categories focus on how people do work.
  - All or some of fifty-four pairs, each consisting of a State Progress category and a State Styles category

Actions

People do the following.
- For each of various *categories for topics*, list (as *topics for evaluation*) elements of work that fit the *category*.
- For each of various elements of work, do the following.
  - Study the extent to which people like doing (or say they like doing) the work.
  - Study the extent to which people dislike doing (or say they dislike doing) the work.
- For each of various *categories of topics*, develop and summarize *findings*.
- Generalize the *findings*.

Remarks

This example features using two rows in Figure 58.
- The group of rows associated with State Progress as a *basis for categories* contains one of these rows.
  - (See the last row in that group.)
- The group of rows associated with State Styles as a *basis for categories* contains one of these rows.
  - (See the last row in that group.)
- Each of the two rows has "Attitudes" as its *facet being measured*.
- Each of the two rows has "Attitudes regarding types of work" as its *theme for evaluation*.

Example: Evaluate marketing themes

This example shows how people can use State Progress as a *basis for categories* for evaluating *marketing themes*, with respect to audiences (a *theme for evaluations*).

Situation

A corporation has a company-wide grassroots innovation program based in part on a new type of computer technology. The program-leading staff function wants to enhance program marketing. The group wants to evaluate potential marketing themes.

Create Metrics

The following pertain.
- *Endeavor*: The program's marketing efforts
- *Facet being measured*: Marketing themes
- *Theme for evaluations*: Marketing themes, with respect to audiences
- *Themes for metrics*: Matches and mismatches between themes in messages and audiences for messages
- *Basis for categories*: State Progress
- *Categories for topics*: All or some of the nine State Progress categories

Actions

The group can do the following.
- Determine potential audiences to which to market.
  - Use the State Synergies checklist.
    - Define the *endeavor* as *the program moves forward (in the context that the corporation operates)*.
  - Determine audience segments.
    - Each segment consists of a person or a group of people having similar interests.
- For each of various *categories for topics* (the selected State Progress categories), think of and list (as *topics for evaluation*) possible marketing themes that fit the *category*.
- For each of various segments, do the following.
  - For each of various possible marketing themes, estimate personal interest in hearing about the theme. Determine matches and mismatches (the *themes for metrics*). Possibly, do the following.
    - Use surveys or focus groups.
    - Use other knowledge or assumptions about the segment.
  - Summarize *findings* relevant to various *categories for topics* (State Progress categories).
  - Determine, from the summarized findings, the extent to which people in the segment likely have interests in various *categories for topics* (State Progress categories).
- Consider redefining segments (based on *findings*) and backtracking (with respect to these *Actions*).
- For each of various segments, do the following.
  - Draft marketing messages that emphasize themes in high-potential *categories for topics* (State Progress categories).

Results

People have candidate marketing messages.

Remarks

This example features using one row in Figure 58.
- The group of rows associated with State Progress as a *basis for categories* contains this row.
- This row has "Marketing themes" as its *facet being measured*.
- This row has "Marketing themes, with respect to audiences" as its *theme for evaluations*.

Example: Facets, evaluation topics, metrics themes, and bases for categories

Figure 58 provides some *facets being measured*, *themes for evaluations*, *themes for metrics*, and *bases for categories*. The figure is organized by *bases for categories*. People can do the following.
- Add or change *facets being measured* items.

- Add or change *themes for evaluations* items.
- Add or change *themes for metrics* items.
  - The figure suggests pairs of *themes*.
  - People can add other *themes*.
- When evaluating *topics*, use all or fewer than all of the relevant *themes for metrics*.

Figure 58 Some facets, evaluations themes, metrics themes, and category bases

Facets being Measured	Themes for Evaluations	Themes for Metrics		Bases for Categories
Cooperation	Results of or possibilities for cooperation	Benefits	Negatives	State Synergies
Cooperativeness	Characterizations regarding cooperativeness	Inclusiveness	Isolation	State Synergies
Analyses of scenarios	Emphases when analyzing multiple scenarios	Similarities	Differences	State Impact
Evaluation of scenarios	Criteria used for evaluating scenarios	Relative	Absolute	State Impact
Evaluation of scenarios	Criteria used for evaluating scenarios	Qualitative	Quantitative	State Impact
Thinking or discussion	Foci of thinking or discussion	Clients	Providers	State Progress
Thinking or discussion	Foci of thinking or discussion	Outcomes	Inputs	State Progress
Thinking or discussion	Foci of thinking or discussion	Benefits	Costs	State Progress
Services	Services, with respect to needs of a client	Outcomes	Inputs	State Progress
Contributions of staff functions	Corporate view of staff-function contributions	Results	Resources	State Progress
Marketing themes	Marketing themes, with respect to audiences	Match	Mismatch	State Progress
Marketing themes	Marketing themes, with respect to services	Match	Mismatch	State Progress
Actions, plans, or histories	Thoroughness of actions, plans, or histories	Complete	Incomplete	State Progress
Attitudes	Attitudes regarding types of work	Likes	Dislikes	State Progress
Teamwork	Work styles, with respect to teamwork	Appropriate	Inappropriate	State Styles
Work	Work styles, with respect to work	Appropriate	Inappropriate	State Styles
Needs for work	Methods, with respect to needs for work	Match	Mismatch	State Styles

Create Metrics

Facets being Measured	Themes for Evaluations	Themes for Metrics		Bases for Categories
Work cultures	Goals or attributes of work cultures	Efficiency	Spontaneity	State Styles
Attitudes	Attitudes regarding types of work	Likes	Dislikes	State Styles
Principles, goals, or incentives	Availability of principles, goals, or incentives	Stated	Unstated	State Purposes
Principles, goals, or incentives	Consistency of principles, goals, or incentives	Aligned	Divergent	State Purposes
Services	Satisfaction, with respect to needs of a client	Match	Mismatch	State Purposes
Marketing themes	Marketing themes, with respect to a client	Match	Mismatch	State Purposes
Marketing themes	Marketing themes, with respect to a provider	Match	Mismatch	State Purposes
Commitment	Level of commitment	Enthused	Ambivalent	State Purposes
Decision-making	Approaches to decision-making	Conscious	Unconscious	State Assumptions
Information	Usefulness of information	Substantiated	Unsubstantiated	State Assumptions
Information usage	Bases for information used	Evidence	Opinion	State Assumptions
Information usage	Potential to study information usage	Supported	Lacking	State Assumptions
Working relationships	Bases for working relationships	Documented	Tacit	State Teamwork
Working relationships	Bases for working relationships	Harmony	Discord	State Teamwork
Knowledge supporting teamwork	Degree of knowledge about an entity	Transparency	Mystery	State Teamwork
Teamwork	Potential for successful teamwork	Positives	Negatives	State Tendencies
Conflicts	Knowledge of conflicts	Appropriate	Inappropriate	State Tendencies
Innovations	Actual or perceived innovations	Innovations	Concepts	State Inventiveness
Innovation	Roles regarding innovation	Comprehensive	Lacking	State Inventiveness
Innovation	Roles regarding innovation	Appropriate	Inappropriate	State Inventiveness
Attitudes	Attitudes regarding types of work	Likes	Dislikes	State Inventiveness
Successfulness	Actual or perceived successfulness	Leading	Trailing	State Drive
Dedication	Actual or perceived dedication to efforts	Diligent	Laidback	State Drive

Facets being Measured	Themes for Evaluations	Themes for Metrics		Bases for Categories
Successfulness and dedication	Historical course of success and dedication	Improving	Worsening	State Drive
Resources	Resources, with respect to an endeavor	Match	Mismatch	State Resources
Resources	Attributes or appropriateness of resources	Strengths	Weaknesses	State Resources
Resources	Foci when gathering resources	Needs	Perceptions	State Resources
				[Other basis]

Perspective

When selecting or using categories based on a Direct Outcomes checklist, people can take into account that both benefits and negatives may pertain for each of the checklist's categories. For example,
- For each State Styles category, Figure 59 suggests possible benefits and negatives. Other benefits and negatives may pertain to an activity or in general.

Figure 59 Some benefits and some negatives of styles of work

Styles	Possible Benefits	Possible Negatives
Effortless / Transcend …	Focus on other activities.	Lack abilities to oversee or perform similar activities.
Embedded / Blend …	Work efficiently on interrelated activities.	Lack abilities to untangle or separate integrated processes.
Procedural / Follow …	Work efficiently on the activity.	Stifle flexibility or creativity regarding the activity.
Tentative / Experiment …	Improve processes methodically.	Focus overly on process and not enough on results.
Haphazard / Meander …	Gain from spontaneous creativity.	Lack needed perspective or focus.
Nil / Defer …	Plan or train before doing.	Delay inappropriately.

For the "foci of thinking or discussion" *themes for evaluations* associated in Figure 58 with State Progress (as a *basis for categories*), the following pertain.
- The first *themes for metrics* (clients, outcomes, benefits) more likely correlate better with the Reuses and nearby-Reuses State Progress categories than do the second *themes for metrics* (providers, inputs, costs).
- The second *themes for metrics* more likely correlate better with the Resources and nearby-Resources categories than do the first *themes for metrics*.

Chapter 23 Create Methods

Use Create Methods techniques. Help people create, extend, integrate, and select methods and checklists.

Too often, people miss opportunities to do the following (adequately well or at all).
- Use methods or checklists.
- Create or select apt methods or checklists.
- Extend or integrate skills, methods, or checklists.
- Make skills, methods, or checklists more relevant.
    - For example, make skills (such as reading or writing) more situation-specific.
    - For example, make qualitative methods (such as soft-skills methods) more situation-specific.
- Decide what to quantify.
    - For example, for dashboards or scorecards, decide what to measure.
- Balance quantitative and non-quantitative thinking.
- Achieve results listed in the right column of Figure 60.

Consider using Direct Outcomes and other methods to help capture such opportunities.

Figure 60 Create, extend, integrate, and select methods

With methods such as …	… use Direct Outcomes checklists to …
Strategic, scenario, or tactical planning … Goal setting … Incentive setting … Risk management …	Spot useful issues, problems, or opportunities. Optimize the scope or a statement of an issue, problem, or opportunity. Pinpoint or reduce possible conflicts among goals, plans, and incentives.
Mission-specific programs …	Reuse practices or results beyond the programs.
Project management … Productivity improvement … Process improvement …	Anticipate needed outcomes. Focus on important work. Organize project phases. Complete work by using appropriate work methods.
Habits or strategies general-skills … Systems thinking … Time management … Communication or negotiation skills … Soft skills …	Deploy situation-specific approaches for using or benefiting from skills or methods.
Quantitative methods* … * For example, statistical process control, Six Sigma, scorecards, dashboards, or benchmarking	Decide what to quantify. Select quantification methods. Pinpoint or reduce possible conflicts among goals, plans, and incentives. Involve people not adept at using quantitative methods.
Creativity or problem-solving checklists* … * For example, TRIZ	Turn concepts into bases for innovations. Involve people not adept at using structured methods.
Behavior proclivity analyses …	Understand other types of proclivity.

With methods such as …	… use Direct Outcomes checklists to …
Knowledge usage … Knowledge services … Knowledge management …	Provide context or goals. Design means to qualify information. Design means to find relevant information. Organize information. Design metadata.
Customer relationship management … Supply chain management … E-commerce … Enterprise resources planning … Information systems development … Applications of service science …	Envision, plan, market, develop, deploy, or benefit from client-support programs (and systems) that support client activities that come as close as possible to generating client outcomes.
Speech, writing, or languages … Science, mathematics, history, or other disciplines …	Facilitate communications - for example, across work cultures, languages, or specialties.
Any of the above methods … Direct Outcomes … Metrics related to any of the above …	Develop methods, checklists, or metrics. Anticipate benefits from using methods, checklists, or metrics. Select methods, checklists, or metrics. Design strategies and tactics to foster use of methods, checklists, or metrics. Measure benefits achieved by using methods, checklists, or metrics.

Example: Develop a human-resources method

A hiring manager wants to develop a template that supports developing job descriptions and providing performance reviews. The manager anticipates using job descriptions during the following activities.
- Review employment candidates' experiences.
- Talk with employees.

The manager builds a template like that in Figure 61. The manager uses the following steps.
- Determine clients of the job.
    - Use State Synergies. Set the State Synergies *endeavor* to be *the jobholder performs useful work*.
- For each type of client, determine services the jobholder needs to provide.
    - Use State Progress. Set the State Progress *endeavor* to be *the client tries to achieve Outcomes*.
- Adopt a measuring scale for jobholder proficiency.
    - Use State Styles. Set the State Styles *endeavor* to be *the jobholder performs work*.

Create Methods	97

Figure 61 A template for job descriptions and performance reviews

Endeavor >							
Job description and performance review							
Person or group >							
Dates (as appropriate): Previous > ; Current > ; Future >							

Activity (or Skill)	Defer	Meander	Experiment	Follow	Blend	Transcend	Discussion
Example:			previous	current	future		
Satisfy customers.							
Improve service to customers.							
Propose service improvements.							
Stay informed about customers.							
Update data about customers.							
Do supervisor's work.							
Coach supervisor.							
Do peers' work.							
Coach peers.							
Ensure subordinates' work.							
Ensure suppliers' work.							
Prepare self for the future.							
Benefit society.							
Other (Specify.):							

When using the template, conceptually people can do the following.
- Specify an endeavor (or context).
- Specify a person or group for which to rate performance.
- Specify one or more of the three dates.
- Add, change, or remove items in the *Activity (or Skill)* column.
- Specify more details for items in the *Activity (or Skill)* column.
- Prepare to note characterizations in appropriate grid elements.
  - *Previous* characterizes past behavior.
  - *Current* characterizes current behavior.
  - *Future* characterizes an expectation for future behavior.
- Peg each characterization or expectation to the following.
  - The *activity* or *skill* noted in the relevant row.
  - The corresponding date noted in the *Dates* line in the figure.
- Provide more information, in the *Discussion* column or in grid elements.

Remarks

For Figure 61, a use of State Synergies yields eight types of clients - customers, a supervisor, peers, subordinates, suppliers, the job holder, society, and possibly others. Applications of State Progress involve, respectively, five, two, two, one, one, one, one, and an unknown number of State Progress categories.

State Styles provides a qualitative rigorous basis for productive discussion, planning, incentive setting, measurement, and performance recognition.

The manger may include other metrics.

98   *Create Crucial Insight*

Example: Develop the State Progress checklist

The State Progress checklist reflects a two-step application of a model. The model features the endeavor elements *effects*, *agendas*, and *potential*.

The left half of Figure 62 portrays a win-win relationship between two entities. For example, the entities can be, respectively, a client and a provider. Each entity receives support from the other entity. In this first-step application of the model, the middle agendas bubble symbolizes mutual agendas.

Figure 62 A win-win relationship and themes for State Progress

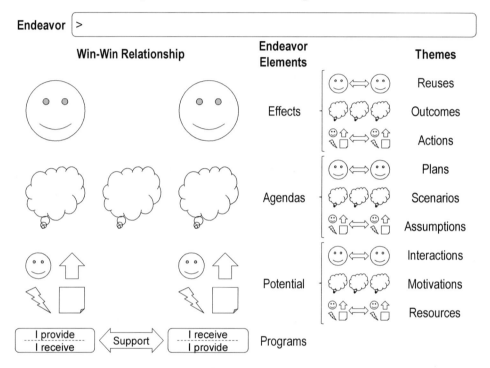

The second-step application of the model treats each of effects, agendas, and potential as having effects, agendas, and potential components. The right half Figure 62 does the following.
- Illustrate this step.
- Show the nine themes that State Progress exhibits.

Remarks

State Progress represents a spectrum of service activities. Figure 62 exhibits a three-band version (*effects*, *agendas*, and *potential*) of the spectrum. The figure also exhibits a nine-band version (*reuses* through *resources*). For a specific use of State Progress, people can adjust the number of bands or the scopes of individual bands.

For any endeavor, people can do the following.
- Plan downward. Potentially, start near the top of the spectrum.
- Adjust plans, based on developments anywhere on the spectrum.
- Realize that successes with lower-on-the-spectrum activities tend to improve possibilities for successes with higher-on-the-spectrum activities.
- Apply State Progress to an activity by considering the activity to be its own endeavor.

Create Methods

The State Assumptions checklist results from the following steps.
- Make a third-step application of the model to State Progress's Assumptions theme.
- Make three partial fourth-step applications that emphasize *effects* and *potential*.

The State Tendencies checklist results from a third-step application of the model to State Progress's Motivations theme.

The State Inventiveness checklist results from considering State Progress's Actions and Motivations themes.

The uppermost State Progress category points toward *possibilities for reuse*. The uppermost State Assumptions category points toward *possibilities for reuse*. The following pertain.
- For State Progress, *reuse* refers to using - outside the endeavor - aspects of the endeavor.
- For State Assumptions, *reuse* refers to using - above (in the sense of the model or the State Progress checklist) State Assumptions - results generated by using State Assumptions.

Figure 63 provides another version of State Progress. This seven-band version and similar versions have carried names including *Achieve Progress*, the *Functionality Scale*, *Select Service*, the *Value Spectrum*, and *Service Value* (as in *value of service*).

Figure 63 A seven-band version of State Progress

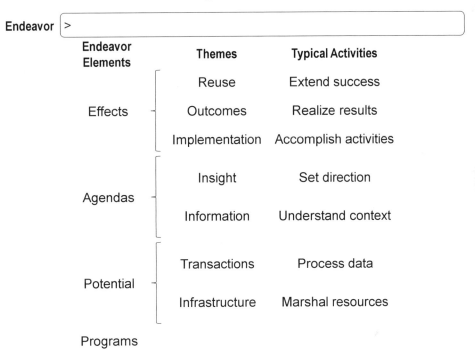

Figure 64 depicts roles regarding knowledge and knowledge services. The roles come from this seven-band version of State Progress.

Figure 64 Roles regarding knowledge

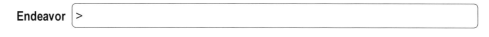

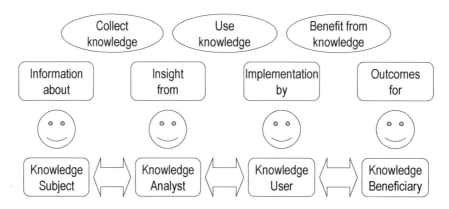

Example: Develop the State Styles checklist

Figure 65 provides a basis for State Styles.

Figure 65 A basis for State Styles

Endeavor >

Analysis of Styles

Analysis of styles, as of (Specify date.) ________________ of the ...

(Select one.)
___ Actual ...
___ Desired ...
___ Other (Specify.) ___________ ...

(Select one.)
___ Approach regarding ...
___ Approach for monitoring effectiveness regarding ...
___ Approach for changing effectiveness regarding ...
___ Approach for (Specify.) ________________________ regarding ...

To what extent does each of these five styles characterize the approach?		Doing the Endeavor	Coordinating the Endeavor with relevant ...					
			Client Endeavors	Peer Endeavors	Provider Endeavors	Past of the Endeavor	Future of the Endeavor	Other Endeavors
(adjective)	(verb)							
Effortless	Transcend							
Procedural	Follow							
Tentative	Experiment							
Haphazard	Meander							
Nil	Defer							

The following remarks pertain.

- The method depicted in Figure 65 is more rigorous than State Styles.
- The list in the lower-left corner lacks State Styles's *Embedded / Blend* category.

Create Methods

- That list and the *Doing the Endeavor* column generate all State Styles categories except the *Embedded / Blend* category.
- The State Styles category *Embedded / Blend* provides an opportunity to address matters corresponding to the rightmost six columns at the bottom of Figure 65.
  – State Synergies provides a basis for those six columns.

The current version and similar versions of State Styles have carried names including *Achieve Style*, the *Proficiency Scale*, *Select Style*, *Style Maturity*, and the *Maturity Spectrum*.

Chapter 24 Meet Author

Learn about this book's author, Dr. Thomas J. Buckholtz.

Tom played pivotal roles in the following endeavors.
- Create lines of business for a $1 billion (annual revenue) business unit.
- Save $100 million per year for a $6 billion company.
- Pioneer three information technologies.
- Establish three information-technology marketplace business practices.
- Develop useful, leading-edge business, engineering, and scientific software.
- Double a two-person firm's revenue, for each of two consecutive years.
- Preserve 7 kilometers of Pacific Ocean coastline.
- Create an international service program.
- Improve governmental service (from all levels of government) for the American public.
- Create a grassroots line-of-business for a United States political party's National Committee.

Tom served in the following capacities.
- Executive leading a $1 billion business unit
- Corporate officer and advisor for startups
- Chief information officer (CIO) for a $10 billion enterprise
- Co-CIO for the United States federal government's Executive Branch
- Program leader advocating innovation, enhancing teamwork, and providing information technology throughout a $6 billion company
- Commissioner, United States General Services Administration
- Mathematician; Scientist; Engineer
- Professorial Lecturer; University Extension Instructor
- Speaker; Workshop provider; Author
- Business advisor; Innovation consultant

Dr. Buckholtz's clients and employers have included large and small enterprises in aerospace, agricultural research, business services, computing, defense, education, energy utilities, government, healthcare, high technology, innovation, insurance, Internet, law enforcement, politics, research and development, telecommunications, and venture capital.

Tom served on elected or appointed boards or in other volunteer capacities for a residential cooperative, a swim club, and organizations in academia, innovation, and public policy. For a successful United States presidential campaign, he served as a donor, fundraiser, policy-research committee member, speaker, alternate delegate at the candidate's party's National Convention, speakers bureau leader, county cochairman, and county representative at regional and statewide meetings. He served as co-producer and co-host for 250 interview-format television programs discussing business, chartable, community, educational, governmental, and political endeavors.

His education includes the following.
- Earn a B.S. in mathematics from the California Institute of Technology.
- Earn a Ph.D. in physics from the University of California, Berkeley.
- Complete business administration programs at Stanford University and the University of Michigan.

Chapter 25   Meet Book

Learn about this book's parts, chapters, chapter summaries, and figures.

Parts, Chapters, Chapter Summaries, and Figures

Preface v
Dedication vii
Acknowledgments vii
Notice viii

Part 1   Get Results 1

   Chapter 1   Meet Insight 3
     Use insight. Thrive. Learn that people use Direct Outcomes checklists to create crucial insight.
       Figure 1   Direct Outcomes themes 3

   Chapter 2   Play 2-Brains 5
     Play a game. Develop themes for marketing messages. Learn how Direct Outcomes can help.
       Figure 2   2-Brains: Tell it & Sell it 5
       Figure 3   Some themes for marketing messages 7
       Figure 4   Some candidates for grid axis labels 8

   Chapter 3   Augment Luck 9
     Anticipate augmenting luck and reducing reliance on luck. Learn how Direct Outcomes can help.
       Figure 5   Luck? Or, Direct Outcomes? 9
       Figure 6   From some questions to some applicable checklists 11
       Figure 7   Results people can achieve by using Direct Outcomes 12

   Chapter 4   Create Insight 13
     Use the Create Insight technique. Create crucial insight. Use Direct Outcomes checklists.
       Figure 8   Create Insight 13
       Figure 9   From some endeavor aspects toward some insights and other results ... 14
       Figure 10   Endeavor themes and some endeavor elements 16
       Figure 11   From endeavor elements to some types of activities 17
       Figure 12   From some types of activities to some applicable checklists 18
       Figure 13   From some endeavor elements to some applicable checklists 19
       Figure 14   Direct Outcomes program principles 20
       Figure 15   From Direct Outcomes themes and book parts to chapters and checklists ... 21
       Figure 16   Structure of a chapter presenting a checklist 22

   Chapter 5   Track Results 23
     Use the Track Results technique. Anticipate and summarize impact of using Direct Outcomes.
       Figure 17   Track Results 23

   Chapter 6   Track Utilization 25
     Use the Track Utilization technique. Anticipate and summarize progress at learning and using Direct Outcomes.
       Figure 18   Track Utilization 25

Part 2	Learn Checklists		27
Chapter 7	State Synergies		29

Use the State Synergies checklist. Spot opportunities for cooperation.

- Figure 19 State Synergies 29
- Figure 20 An application of State Synergies to hiring a salesperson 30
- Figure 21 Interpreting an aspect of a company-wide innovation program 31

Chapter 8 State Impact 33

Use the State Impact checklist. Evaluate courses of action.

- Figure 22 State Impact 33
- Figure 23 An application of State Impact to hiring a salesperson 35
- Figure 24 Interpreting an aspect of a company-wide innovation program 36

Chapter 9 State Progress 37

Use the State Progress checklist. Plan and manage services, programs, and projects. Envision new products and services. Develop marketing themes.

- Figure 25 State Progress 37
- Figure 26 An application of State Progress to hiring a salesperson 39
- Figure 27 Interpreting an aspect of a company-wide innovation program 40

Chapter 10 State Styles 41

Use the State Styles checklist. Analyze how work is or could be done.

- Figure 28 State Styles 41
- Figure 29 An application of State Styles to hiring a salesperson 43
- Figure 30 Interpreting an aspect of a company-wide innovation program 44

Chapter 11 State Purposes 45

Use the State Purposes checklist. Envision purposes that motivate or can motivate individuals, teams, relationships, and activities.

- Figure 31 State Purposes 45
- Figure 32 An application of State Purposes to hiring a salesperson 47
- Figure 33 Interpreting an aspect of a company-wide innovation program 48

Chapter 12 State Assumptions 49

Use the State Assumptions checklist. Determine the extent information meets needs. Spot needs for additional information.

- Figure 34 State Assumptions 49
- Figure 35 An application of State Assumptions to hiring a salesperson 51
- Figure 36 Interpreting an aspect of a company-wide innovation program 52

Chapter 13 State Teamwork 53

Use the State Teamwork checklist. Envision and guide relationships between entities.

- Figure 37 State Teamwork 53
- Figure 38 An application of State Teamwork to hiring a salesperson 55
- Figure 39 Interpreting an aspect of a company-wide innovation program 56

Chapter 14 State Tendencies 57

Use the State Tendencies checklist. Envision matches and mismatches between needs to do work and behaviors people tend to use when working.

- Figure 40 State Tendencies 57
- Figure 41 An application of State Tendencies to hiring a salesperson 59
- Figure 42 Interpreting an aspect of a company-wide innovation program 60

Chapter 15   State Inventiveness 61
    Use the State Inventiveness checklist. Envision matches and mismatches between needs for innovation and proclivities of participants.
        Figure 43   State Inventiveness.. 61
        Figure 44   An application of State Inventiveness to hiring a salesperson.............................. 63
        Figure 45   Interpreting an aspect of a company-wide innovation program......................... 63

Chapter 16   State Drive..65
    Use the State Drive checklist. Envision matches and mismatches between endeavor needs or cultures and participants' attitudes.
        Figure 46   State Drive... 65
        Figure 47   An application of State Drive to hiring a salesperson 67
        Figure 48   Interpreting an aspect of a company-wide innovation program......................... 67

Chapter 17   State Resources...69
    Use the State Resources checklist. Determine capabilities needed so that endeavors succeed.
        Figure 49   State Resources 69
        Figure 50   An application of State Resources to hiring a salesperson 71
        Figure 51   Interpreting an aspect of a company-wide innovation program......................... 72

Part 3   Learn More 73

Chapter 18   Foster Win-Win...75
    Use the Foster Win-Win technique. Help clients and providers optimize results for each other.
        Figure 52   Needs of a client's endeavor... 76
        Figure 53   Activities for a provider... 76

Chapter 19   Detail Opportunities..79
    Use Detail Opportunities information. Gain insight about uses for and origins of Direct Outcomes.

Chapter 20   Describe Capabilities 83
    Use the Describe Capabilities technique. Develop themes for marketing entities' services.
        Figure 54   Describe Capabilities... 83
        Figure 55   From Direct Outcomes checklists to some typical actions 84

Chapter 21   Teach Methods..87
    Use Teach Methods techniques. Help people learn and use work methods and work-improvement methods.
        Figure 56   Learn and benefit from methods 88

Chapter 22   Create Metrics...89
    Use the Create Metrics technique. Help people create and use metrics.
        Figure 57   Create Metrics 89
        Figure 58   Some facets, evaluations themes, metrics themes, and category bases................. 92
        Figure 59   Some benefits and some negatives of styles of work 94

Chapter 23   Create Methods 95
    Use Create Methods techniques. Help people create, extend, integrate, and select methods and checklists.
        Figure 60   Create, extend, integrate, and select methods... 95
        Figure 61   A template for job descriptions and performance reviews.................................... 97
        Figure 62   A win-win relationship and themes for State Progress 98
        Figure 63   A seven-band version of State Progress 99

Figure 64	Roles regarding knowledge	100
Figure 65	A basis for State Styles	100

Chapter 24　Meet Author 103
　　Learn about this book's author, Dr. Thomas J. Buckholtz.

Chapter 25　Meet Book 105
　　Learn about this book's parts, chapters, chapter summaries, and figures.

Made in the USA
Middletown, DE
27 June 2018